by Charles Busch

A SAMUEL FRENCH ACTING EDITION

SAMUEL FRENCH

FOUNDED 1830

New York Hollywood London Toronto

SAMUELFRENCH.COM

ISBN   978-0-573-67027-5   Printed   in   U.S.A.   #18168

MUSIC USE NOTE

Licensees are solely responsible for obtaining formal written permission from copyright owners to use copyrighted music in the performance of this play and are strongly cautioned to do so. If no such permission is obtained by the licensee, then the licensee must use only original music that the licensee owns and controls. Licensees are solely responsible and liable for all music clearances and shall indemnify the copyright owners of the play and their licensing agent, Samuel French, Inc., against any costs, expenses, losses and liabilities arising from the use of music by licensees.

Samuel French, Inc. can supply the recording of the music used in the original Off-Broadway production. Fees quoted upon application.

IMPORTANT BILLING AND CREDIT REQUIREMENTS

All producers of *PSYCHO BEACH PARTY must* give credit to the Author of the Play in all programs distributed in connection with performances of the Play, and in all instances in which the title of the Play appears for the purposes of advertising, publicizing or otherwise exploiting the Play and/or a production. The name of the Author *must* appear on a separate line on which no other name appears, immediately following the title and *must* appear in size of type not less than fifty percent of the size of the title type.

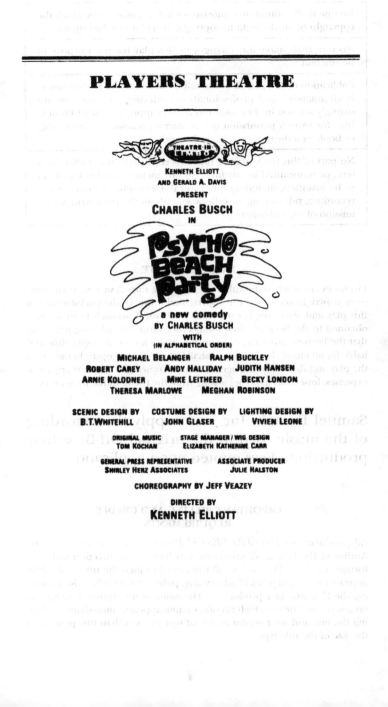

PLAYERS THEATRE

KENNETH ELLIOTT
AND GERALD A. DAVIS

PRESENT

CHARLES BUSCH

IN

Psycho Beach Party

a new comedy
BY CHARLES BUSCH

WITH
(IN ALPHABETICAL ORDER)

MICHAEL BELANGER   RALPH BUCKLEY
ROBERT CAREY   ANDY HALLIDAY   JUDITH HANSEN
ARNIE KOLODNER   MIKE LEITHEED   BECKY LONDON
THERESA MARLOWE   MEGHAN ROBINSON

SCENIC DESIGN BY	COSTUME DESIGN BY	LIGHTING DESIGN BY
B.T. WHITEHILL	JOHN GLASER	VIVIEN LEONE

ORIGINAL MUSIC   STAGE MANAGER / WIG DESIGN
TOM KOCHAN   ELIZABETH KATHERINE CARR

GENERAL PRESS REPRESENTATIVE   ASSOCIATE PRODUCER
SHIRLEY HERZ ASSOCIATES   JULIE HALSTON

CHOREOGRAPHY BY JEFF VEAZEY

DIRECTED BY
KENNETH ELLIOTT

CAST

(in order of appearance)

Yo-Yo . . . . ROBERT CAREY

Dee Dee . . . . JUDITH HANSEN

Nicky . . . . MIKE LEITHEED

Provoloney . . . . ANDY HALLIDAY

Star Cat . . . . ARNIE KOLODNER

Chicklet . . . . CHARLES BUSCH

Kanaka . . . . RALPH BUCKLEY

Berdine . . . . BECKY LONDON

Marvel Ann . . . . MICHAEL BELANGER

Mrs. Forrest . . . . MEGHAN ROBINSON

Bettina Barnes . . . . THERESA MARLOWE

The action takes place on and around a beach in Malibu, 1962

THE PLAY WILL BE PERFORMED WITHOUT AN INTERMISSION

UNDERSTUDIES

Understudies never substitute for listed players unless a specific announcement
for the appearance is made at the time of the performance.

JUDITH HANSEN for Mr. Belanger, Ms. London, Ms. Robinson, Ms. Marlowe.
LAURENCE OVERMIRE for Mr. Buckley, Mr. Carey, Mr. Halliday,
Mr. Kolodner and Mr. Leitheed.

"Chicklet" love theme sung by Michael Maguire.

Lyrics by Ken Elliott.

CAST

Yo-Yo
Dee Dee
Nicky
Provoloney
Star Cat
Chicklet
Kanaka
Berdine
Marvel Ann
Mrs. Forrest
Bettina Barnes

PLACE

On and around a beach in Malibu.

TIME

1962

Theatre-in-Limbo, Kenneth Elliott and Gerald A. Davis presented PSYCHO BEACH PARTY on July 20, 1987 at the Players Theatre, New York City. The cast was as follows:

YO-YO............................... Robert Carey
DEE DEE ....Judith Hansen
NICKY............................... Mike Leitheed
PROVOLONEY.................... Andy Halliday
STAR CAT .... Arnie Koldner
CHICKLET........................ Charles Busch
KANAKA .... Ralph Buckley
BERDINE.......................... Becky London
MARVEL ANN................... Michael Belanger
MRS. FORREST .... Meghan Robinson
BETTINA BARNES .... Theresa Marlowe
SWING/UNDERSTUDY .... Laurence Overmire

Scenic Design .... B.T. Whitehill
Costume Design..................... John Glaser
Lighting Design .... Vivien Leone
Production Stage Manager/
   Wig Design.............. Elizabeth Katherine Carr
Original Music .... Tom Kochan
Production Advisor .... T.L. Boston
Associate Producers...................Julie Halston
                                    Mario Andriolo
Choreography .... Jeff Veazey
Directed by .... Kenneth Elliott

The play was previously presented at the Limbo Lounge in New York City, in October, 1986.

AUTHOR'S NOTES

Why would anyone want to write a spoof of beach party movies? Well, for one thing, the original "Gidget" movie is not bad. It's not "Le Grand Illusion," but it is fun and insightful, and the movie's star, Sandra Dee, I believe is a much-maligned talent. Still, a parody of 1960's teen exploitation flicks would seem to be rather thin stuff. I confess, I began writing this play with a fairly crass motive. I needed a vehicle for my theatrical troupe, Theatre-in-Limbo, to perform as a midnight show. One night over pepperoni pizza, off the top of my head, I came out with the title "Gidget Goes Psychotic." I knew right away that that title would pull in our cult audience in droves. You see what I mean, pretty crass thinking.

However, I found while I was writing that by placing Gidget into the genre of psychological melodrama such as "The Three Faces of Eve," "Suddenly Last Summer" and "Spellbound," I was developing something far more interesting. The movie parody was merely a starting off point for me to write something rather personal and reflective. I'm hardly attributing Beckettian resonances to "Psycho Beach Party" but I like to think there is more to it than meets the eye. Eventually, I changed the title because I felt "Gidget Goes Psychotic" too specific and limiting.

We found it best to act the play very "straight" and uncampy but in a heightened emotional style. Some of the biggest laughs came about by an actor reacting in a harrowingly intense manner which was unfortunately inappropriate to the situation. In the original production, I played Chicklet in drag and another fella, Michael Belanger, played Marvel Ann. We tried to play these female roles with total conviction, finding humor in the reality of the character. I don't think it's necessary for men to play these female roles. In fact, my understudy was a girl and played the role very successfully. It was a cruel awakening because I was so sure that I was irreplaceable. I guess you can't be sure of anything in this world. Nothing is what it seems. Like, hey, maybe that's what this play's all about.

PRODUCTION NOTES

Pace is very important to the success of PSYCHO BEACH PARTY. Movement from scene to scene should be fast, in the manner of cinematic quick cuts. Long scene changes will destroy the fluidity of the show.

Although the show is set in a number of locations in and around Malibu, the setting for the New York production was extremely simple. It consisted of a series of decorative portals and a backdrop framing a bare stage. Changes in time and locale were indicated mostly through lighting. There were additional set pieces for some of the scenes which were easily and quickly swung into place. For the last scene, a romantic roll drop depicting a sunset over the Pacific was brought in. Details are provided in the groundplan at the back of this book.

Music is an important element of the show for bridges, underscoring, and musical numbers. The "Luau" scene should open with a wild limbo number. Obviously, the music should be of the early sixties period. Some of the show music from the New York production is available for rental from Samuel French, Inc. But regardless of whether you use the original music or choose your own, it should be remembered that music will help give the show a period flavor and an energetic feeling.

PSYCHO BEACH PARTY

SCENE ONE

*Malibu Beach, 1962. Two handsome, young beach bums named
YO YO and NICKY, and a sexy chick in a bikini named
DEE DEE, are madly cavorting with a beach ball.*

Yo Yo. *(To DEE DEE)* Baby, shake those maracas.
Dee Dee. *(Squeals)* Stop teasing me, Yo Yo.
Nicky. Look at that butt.
Dee Dee. You guys have a one track mind.

*(PROVOLONEY, a scrappy, little surfer, the joker of the group,
runs on.)*

Provoloney. Girls! Girls! Girls!
Yo Yo. Hey there, Provoloney!
Nicky. and Dee Dee. Hi, Provoloney.
Provoloney. What a fantabulous day.
Dee Dee. Gosh, I love the sun.
Nicky. Aw shoot, we've got to get back to the malt
shop. Our lunch break is almost over.
Yo Yo. Call in sick.
Provoloney. Say you were run over by a hit-and-
run surfer.
Nicky. Nah, old Augie's a great guy. I couldn't let
him down.

11

DEE DEE. Gosh, I really love him.

(STARCAT, the most handsome of the group, enters with a surf board.)

YO YO. Hey, Star Cat, how's my man?

STAR CAT. What are you clowns doing? Those waves are as high as Mount Everest.

PROVOLONEY. *(Looks out)* Oh wow, look at them, man.

STAR CAT. It's time to hit the water.

NICKY. It's more BLT's for us. Let's hit the road, Dee Dee.

DEE DEE. Sure thing. Gosh, I'm so happy. *(THEY exit.)*

BOYS. Bye!

STAR CAT. Come on guys, grab your boards, it's time to shoot the curl.

PROVOLONEY. Hot diggity! *(THEY all run offstage.)*

(CHICKLET, a perky, fifteen-year-old girl skips on.)

CHICKLET. *(To the audience)* Hi folks, welcome to Malibu Beach. I hope you brought your suntan lotion cause here it's what you call endless summer. My name's Chicklet. Sort of a kooky name and believe me, it has nothing to do with chewing gum. You see, I've always been so darn skinny, a stick, a shrimp, so when other girls turned into gorgeous chicks, I became a chicklet. Can't say I've always been thrilled with that particular nomenclature but it sure beats the heck out of my real name,

Florence. I'm supposed to meet my girlfriends, Marvel Ann and Berdine here at the beach. Marvel Ann calls it a "man hunt." I don't know what's wrong with me. I like boys, but not when they get all icky and unglued over you. All that kissy kissy stuff just sticks in my craw. I don't know, maybe I need some hormone shots. I do have a deep, all-consuming passion. The mere thought fills me with tingles and ecstasy. It's for surfing. I'm absolutely flaked out about riding the waves. Of course, I don't know how to do it, not yet, but I'm scouting around for a teacher and when I do, look out world. You'll be seeing old Chicklet flying over those waves like a comet.

(KANAKA, the macho king of the surfers, enters, drinking from a coffee mug.)

CHICKLET. I can't believe it. You're the great Kanaka, aren't you?

KANAKA. Yes, I am the party to whom you are genuflecting.

CHICKLET. Oh gosh, I'm just like your biggest fan. I was standing down front during the surfing competition—

KANAKA. Hey, cool down. Pour some water on that carburetor.

CHICKLET. I haven't even introduced myself, I'm Chicklet Forrest. You're like a living legend. Did you really ride the killer wave off the coast of Bali?

KANAKA. In handcuffs. So how come you know so much about surfing?

CHICKLET. I don't but I'm dying to learn.

KANAKA. A girl surfer? That's like a bad joke.

CHICKLET. Why? Couldn't you teach me? I'm a great swimmer.

KANAKA. You're a tadpole. You're not meant to hit the high waves. It's like a mystical calling. Sorry, babe, sign up with the YMCA.

CHICKLET. But Kanaka...

KANAKA. Hey, little girl. I'm drinking my morning java, my grey cells are still dozing, in other words, angel, buzz off.

BERDINE. *(Offstage)* Chicklet! Come on!

CHICKLET. Well, you haven't heard the last of me. You'll see, I'm going to be your greatest student if it kills you. Tootles. *(SHE exits.)*

(STAR CAT, YO YO and PROVOLONEY run on, excited.)

STAR CAT. Hey Kanaka! You won't believe what's going on.

PROVOLONEY. I swear Malibu Mac is going to kill the joker.

KANAKA. I'm trying to drink my mother lovin java...

YO YO. Didn't you see the cop cars down the beach?

KANAKA. *(Sees them.)* Oh yeah, what's happening?

STAR CAT. It's like a bad dream. Malibu Mac has been dating that high school chick, Beverly Jo.

KANAKA. The homecoming queen, right?

PROVOLONEY. They spent the night on the beach.

YO YO. They were knocked out cold.

STAR CAT. This morning they woke up, naked as they

were born and some weirdo had shaved their bodies head to toe.

Yo Yo. Not a whisker on 'em. Twin bowling balls.

KANAKA. And Malibu Mac had a thing about his pompadour.

PROVOLONEY. He looks like a six-foot wiener.

Yo Yo. Talking about wieners, my stomach's saying "Feed me."

STAR CAT. You're always stuffing your face.

Yo Yo. Food is my hobby.

PROVOLONEY. Yo Yo's a great chef. We've set up like a whole kitchen in our beach shack.

KANAKA. Our beach shack? I never heard of two surf bums shacking up together.

PROVOLONEY. You should see how Yo Yo has fixed up the place with fishnet curtains, rattan furniture, hanging plants.

KANAKA. Hanging plants?

Yo Yo. (Innocently) I do wonderful things with Hibithcuth. (THEY all do a take.)

PROVOLONEY. My innards are screaming "chow."

Yo Yo. Mine are screaming "give me chile dogs!"

STAR CAT. See you clowns later.

PROVOLONEY. (Exiting with YO YO.) Food! Food! Food! (THEY exit.)

STAR CAT. Kanaka, I talked to my dad yesterday.

KANAKA. Yeah?

STAR CAT. I told him I wasn't going back to college. This pre-med stuff is for squares.

KANAKA. But I thought you wanted to be a psychiatrist.

STAR CAT. I was a kid. Now I know I want to be a surf bum. My dad hit the roof but he doesn't understand. He grew up dirt poor and made his money tooth and nail. I can't compete with that. More than anything I want his respect and I'll get that by bumming around with you.

KANAKA. But you know, being a surf bum is a tall order. Only a few make the grade. It's like being a high priest, kinda. No involvements, no commitments, just following the sun. You gotta be a man.

STAR CAT. I swear I won't let you down.

KANAKA. You're a good guy, Star Cat. I think this is the time I show you some of my treasures. I got in my shack a necklace composed of genuine human eyeballs presented to the great Kanaka by a witch doctor in Peru.

STAR CAT. Oh wow!

KANAKA. Let's go. *(THEY exit.)*

(MARVEL ANN and BERDINE enter carrying beach bags. MARVEL ANN is a gorgeous blonde high school vamp and BERDINE is a hopeless nerd, but a nerd with spunk.)

MARVEL ANN. Honestly Berdine, did you have to put that disgusting white gook all over your nose?

BERDINE. Sorry, Marvel Ann, but I got this allergy that flares up whenever I go to the beach.

MARVEL ANN. What are you allergic to?

BERDINE. The sun. It's ghastly. My face turns beet red, my eyes close up, and I get this terrible chafing between my legs.

MARVEL ANN. Charming. Help me spread out the

blanket. *(THEY do.)*

BERDINE. Marvel Ann, this blanket is really divoon.

MARVEL ANN. It's coordinated with my skin tone. Chicklet, help us.

(CHICKLET enters.)

CHICKLET. I found something in the sand.

BERDINE. What is it, a shell?

CHICKLET. No look. *(SHE dangles a spider in front of Marvel Ann.)*

MARVEL ANN. *(Screams in terror.)* A black widow! *(SHE pushes it out of Chicklet's hand.)*

CHICKLET. You scared it.

MARVEL ANN. Listen you two weirdos, my nerves are a frazzle. I can't believe what happened to Beverly Jo. I'm going to have nightmares all night from seeing her like that.

BERDINE. I wonder what the penalty is for shaving someone's head.

CHICKLET. It wasn't just her head. Couldn't you see, they also shaved her... *(SHE whispers "pussy" in Berdine's ear and THEY are dissolved in giggles.)*

MARVEL ANN. Cut that out. I think you two have forgotten the reason we're here. This is a man hunt, capiche?

CHICKLET. Why do we have to bother with them? Can't we just have a good time by ourselves?

MARVEL ANN. You have a severe problem, Chicklet. You've got the sex drive of a marshmallow, you're pushing sixteen. So what if you're an A student, that's parent's stuff. Get with it.

CHICKLET. Maybe I'm just some kind of a freak. Maybe I'll never fall in love.

BERDINE. Oh you will, you will.

CHICKLET. But how will I know when it hits me?

BERDINE. You will, you will.

MARVEL ANN. Chicklet, what are you trying to do, spoil the picture? Take off your top. You've got your swim suit on, don't you? Peel, girl, peel.

CHICKLET. Darn it, it's in my bag and there's no ladies room to change in.

MARVEL ANN. There's no one around. You better hurry.

BERDINE. You can't take your top off here.

CHICKLET. Hold the blanket up and no one will see me. *(THEY hold up the blanket, CHICKLET takes off her smock, revealing her nude, flat chest.)* I'm hopeless. I'm built just like a boy. I wonder if I'll ever fill out.

BERDINE. Hurry up, Chicklet. Marvel Ann, hold the blanket up so I can help Chicklet with her top. *(CHICKLET pulls on her bathing suit top.)*

MARVEL ANN. We're in luck. Look at those four gorgeous hunks of male, over there, almost enough for second helpings. Now a manuever like this takes technique. Talk to me. Don't let them think we're looking at them.

CHICKLET. What should we talk about?

MARVEL ANN. Anything.

BERDINE. I'm reading the most exciting book. It's by Jean Paul Sartre. It's called "Nausea."

MARVEL ANN. *(Posing and not paying attention.)* Oh,

really.

BERDINE. It's the most clear-headed explanation of existentialism. The whole concept of free will being conscious choice against the determining...

MARVEL ANN. *(With extreme bitchiness)* I'll see the movie.

CHICKLET. Gosh, Berdine, I'm impressed. You're a real egghead.

MARVEL ANN. They're looking this way. Now very slowly, let's turn our heads in their direction. *(THEY simultaneously turn their heads.)* Slowly. Cock your head to the side and give a little smile. *(THEY cock their heads and smile in unison.)* Not like that, Berdine, you look like you've got whiplash. *(BERDINE straightens up.)* The blonde one is giggling. *(SHE giggles.)*

CHICKLET. What's so funny?

MARVEL ANN. Shut up. Now we go in for the kill. *(SHE makes a sexy growl.)*

CHICKLET. What's she doing now?

BERDINE. I believe she's displaying animal magnetism. *(BERDINE and CHICKLET start growling and barking like wild dogs and apes.)*

MARVEL ANN. What the hell are you two doing? Oh, now you've done it. They're laughing at us. How dare you. I hate you both.

CHICKLET. Marvel Ann, don't lose your sense of humor.

MARVEL ANN. *(Stands up.)* Oh, I'm laughing all right and so is everyone else at school, laughing at how backward you are. I ought to get the purple heart just for being seen with you. *(Turns to leave.)*

BERDINE. Where are you going?

MARVEL ANN. I didn't come to the beach to play. I came here to catch a man. So if you'll excuse me, I think I'll set my traps elsewhere.

CHICKLET. Can we come too?

MARVEL ANN. What's the point in meeting boys? You two queerbaits should get a license and marry each other. *(SHE exits, laughing.)*

CHICKLET. What sort of nasty crack is that?

BERDINE. I don't see anything wrong with having a best friend.

CHICKLET. I suppose some friends get so close that they lose their individual identities.

BERDINE. We're two very independent personalities.

CHICKLET. She's just jealous cause...

BERDINE. *(Finishing her sentence.)* We've never really accepted her. How could we, she's...

CHICKLET. dumb as a stick. I don't think she's ever read a book...

BERDINE. all the way to the end. Someday she'll be sorry...

CHICKLET. that she rushed into adulthood. We're much wiser to

BERDINE/CHICKLET. *(Simultaneously)* take our time.

CHICKLET. I don't think virginity is such a horrible...

BERDINE. degrading...

CHICKLET. awful thing. You know of course what she did with you know who in the...

BERDINE. *(Understands perfectly.)* Uh huh. Uh huh. And did you know she...

CHICKLET. *(Understands perfectly.)* Uh huh. But I think there's more to it. I think, well ... you know...

BERDINE. Really? *(Giggles.)*

CHICKLET. It reminds me of that book we read, what was it?

BERDINE. *(Knows the book.)* Yes, yes, yes. That's exactly the same kinda...

CHICKLET. And look what ... well...

BERDINE. So true, so true. I couldn't have said it better myself.

(MARVEL ANN enters with KANAKA and STAR CAT.)

MARVEL ANN. Look what I found in the sand. Two hunks of California he-man.

KANAKA. I dig a mermaid whose lips are as flip as her fins.

MARVEL ANN. *(Coyly)* Don't swim too fast upstream, you can still lose the race.

KANAKA. I know how to glide on wave power when I have to.

STAR CAT. *(To Marvel Ann)* Hey, the waves are flipping out. Come and watch me surf standing on my head.

CHICKLET. *(Wildly impressed)* Can you really do that?

STAR CAT. Sure. *(To Marvel Ann)* I can do lots of special tricks.

CHICKLET. *(Innocently)* Really? Like what?

STAR CAT. *(To Marvel Ann)* You interested?

MARVEL ANN. *(Provocatively)* Very interested.

CHICKLET. *(Thinks they're talking about surfing.)* So am I. Let's go right now.

MARVEL ANN. I'd rather see you try those stunts on land.

CHICKLET. That's not the same thing at all.

MARVEL ANN. I missed your name, tall, dark and brooding.

STAR CAT. They call me Star Cat.

MARVEL ANN. I call you cute.

STAR CAT. I'd like to call you sometime.

MARVEL ANN. I'm in the phone book under my father's name, Franklin McCallister, I'm Marvel Ann.

CHICKLET. You can call me too. I'm Chicklet. Here. I'll write down my number cause golly, I'd do anything to see you surf standing on your...

MARVEL ANN. Oh pooh, the sun's playing hookey. No use sitting around here.

KANAKA. Star Cat, let's help the lady.

STAR CAT. You bet!

MARVEL ANN. *(SHE holds up the blanket, the BOYS help her.)* Why thank you, gentlemen. Come, girls.

CHICKLET. That's okay, Marvel Ann. I think I'll stay out a little longer. I'll call you when I get home, Berdine. Okle dokle?

BERDINE. *(Wary)* Okle dokle.

MARVEL ANN. *(Suspiciously)* Okle dokle. *(THEY exit.)*

KANAKA. *(To Star Cat)* Good going, pal. I bet she's hot and spicy between the enchilada.

CHICKLET. If Kanaka won't teach me to surf, will you? I'm a quick study. Straight A's in all my classes.

STAR CAT. You think I'm impressed? Listen little girl, surfing is a man's work. Be a girl. You're more fish than dish. Me teach you how to surf? Don't make me laugh.

I'd rather teach a chicken to lay an elephant's turd. Go home to mama and run, don't walk. *(HE exits.)*

CHICKLET. Boy, he's a grump.

KANAKA. Aw, Star Cat's a raw pearl. He's just a sensitive kind of fella. Hey, look at that kite.

CHICKLET. Which one?

KANAKA. The red one with the flying fish.

(CHICKLET'S face becomes distorted and she becomes her alter ego, ANN BOWMAN, a glamorous femme fatale.)

KANAKA. *(Oblivious)* When I was a kid, I was bananas over flying kites. More than anything, I'd like to be running with a kite against the wind.

CHICKLET. *(Laughs)* Darling, more than anything, I'd like a cool martini, dry with a twist.

KANAKA. Say what?

CHICKLET. You do know what a martini is, my delicious Neanderthal.

KANAKA. Chicklet?

CHICKLET. *(Laughs)* I'm afraid you've got the wrong girl. Chicklet is not my name.

KANAKA. Who are you?

CHICKLET. My name is Ann Bowman.

KANAKA. *(Laughs)* That's pretty good. You wanna be an actress?

CHICKLET. I'm revealing my true nature. *(Fingers his fly.)* I'd like to see you strip down to your truest self.

KANAKA. *(Pushes her hand away.)* Hey, you shouldn't do that.

CHICKLET. Give me one good reason.

KANAKA. You're underage.

CHICKLET. My energy is as old as the Incan temples. You ever been to Peru, baby?

KANAKA. Can't say I have.

CHICKLET. Someday, you and I must explore the ancient temple of Aca Jo Tep. But enough about that for now, what about us?

KANAKA. Hey, cool your jets, babe. If I didn't live by my personal code of honor, I might take advantage of this situation erotically, as it were.

CHICKLET. Give into the feeling, Daddy-O.

KANAKA. Cut the soundtrack for a minute and listen up. Let me give you the number one rule of sexual relations. No stud digs a heavy come-on from a babe. A chick can play it tough but underneath the makeup, a dude's gotta know the chick's a lady. In straight lingo, no pigs need apply.

CHICKLET. (Lies on the ground) Forget the rules, lie here on the sand with me. Doncha love the feel of hot sand against your nude flesh?

KANAKA. I don't know what you're up to but you've got the wrong hep cat.

CHICKLET. Perhaps I do. I thought you were the man with the big cigar. What are you packing, a tiparillo?

KANAKA. More than you can handle, kid. They ought to send you to the juvenile detention hall.

CHICKLET. Aw, I'm scaring the "wittle" boy.

KANAKA. Doll, when I dance, I make the moves, the chick always follows. (HE turns to leave)

CHICKLET. (With mad ferocity) Don't you turn your butt to me!

KANAKA. *(Turns around shocked)* Chicklet?

CHICKLET. I am not Chicklet, you lobotomized numbskull!!!

KANAKA. C'mon stop fooling.

CHICKLET. Do not test me. I will have my way. *(Laughs)* I frighten you, don't I?

KANAKA. No, I ain't scared.

CHICKLET. You're lying. You're yellow as a traffic light, you sniveling little prick. You're scared.

KANAKA. No.

CHICKLET. Look at your hands, they're shaking like jello.

KANAKA. *(Hides his hands)* No, they ain't.

CHICKLET. You're scared. Say it, you're scared.

KANAKA. Yes!

CHICKLET. Yes what?

KANAKA. Yes, ma'am.

CHICKLET. Ah, that's better. You're just a little slave boy, aren't you, sonny?

KANAKA. I gotta get outta here.

CHICKLET. You ain't going anywhere, punk. You know, I'm going to give you what you always wanted.

KANAKA. You are?

CHICKLET. I think we understand each other very well. I know what you fantasize about, I know what you dream about and I'm going to give it to you in spades. Now I want you to go into town and buy yourself a slave collar and a garter belt and a pair of black silk stockings. Spike heels will complete the ensemble and then my dear darling Kanaka, I'm gonna shave all that man fur off you and you'll look just like the little boy that you are.

KANAKA. But what will the rest of the fellas think?

CHICKLET. *(In a rage)* To hell with the rest of the fellas! I am the most important! Me! Ann Bowman! I will not be cast aside, I will not be... *(Becomes CHICKLET again)* Of course, my Mom's an old prude, she won't think surfing is ladylike but I know I can win her over.

KANAKA. *(In shock)* What?

CHICKLET. My Mom. I'm gonna have to ask her permission.

KANAKA. Ann?

CHICKLET. My name's Chicklet, silly. So are you gonna teach me, please, please, pretty please.

KANAKA. Do you remember what we were just talking about?

CHICKLET. Surfing lessons.

KANAKA. No after that, I mean before that.

CHICKLET. Your friend Star Cat? I'm wearing down you resistance, aren't I?

KANAKA. *(Very confused)* Yeah, I'll say.

CHICKLET. Can we start tomorrow?

KANAKA. Yeah, sure.

CHICKLET. Yippee! I gotta get moving, gotta round up a board, get my Mom's okay and then tomorrow, we hit the old H2O. Tootles. *(SHE exits)*

KANAKA. *(Scratching his head in disbelief)* A red kite with a flying fish.

BLACKOUT

SCENE TWO

(Chicklet's house. SHE enters)

CHICKLET. Mom, I'm home. Gosh, the place looks spotless. Was Sadie here today?

(MRS. FORREST enters, the spitting image of Joan Crawford.)

MRS. FORREST. Unfortunately no. Poor Sadie's brother Bubba was run over by a hit-and-run driver. You know our Sadie, always an excuse not to work. I've been on my hands and knees scrubbing all morning. And to top it off, I was experimenting cooking a veal scallopini in the pressure cooker. The darn thing exploded and I'm still finding bits of scallopini in my wiglet.

CHICKLET. Well, the house looks swell.

MRS. FORREST. Thank you, dear. Did you enjoy yourself at the beach? *(Puts arm around her)*

CHICKLET. I guess so.

MRS. FORREST. I detect a sphinx-like expression. Penny for your thoughts.

CHICKLET. *(Looking for a way to tell her about surfing)* I just hate thinking of you doing all that nasty housework. You're so beautiful.

MRS. FORREST. *(Laughs)* My darling daughter, I am just an old widow and a little hard work never hurt anyone.

27

CHICKLET. You're still young. Haven't you ever thought of remarrying?

MRS. FORREST. Your father was the great love of my life. I've always regretted that he died before you were born, that you never knew him. He was quite a guy. A damn good provider. And, darling, to even think of another man would betray his memory.

CHICKLET. I really love you but I don't think I'm pulling my weight around here. I've been thinking, there must be more chores for me to do, painting the inside of the trash cans, polishing the cactus plants.

MRS. FORREST. Chicklet, I smell a rat.

CHICKLET. I'll exterminate it.

MRS. FORREST. Chicklet, what's going on up there in the old attic? (Indicating her brain)

CHICKLET. Okay, Mom, cards on the table. I need twenty-five dollars to buy a surf board.

MRS. FORREST. Out of the question.

CHICKLET. Mom, it's the chance of a lifetime. The great Kanaka has promised to teach me to surf.

MRS. FORREST. The great who?

CHICKLET. The great Kanaka, why he's practically as famous as the President of the United States.

MRS. FORREST. It's too dangerous.

CHICKLET. It's as safe as playing jacks. Please let me Mom. It'll be sheer heaven or months and months of stark solitude.

MRS. FORREST. I will not have my daughter cavorting with a band of derelict beach bums.

CHICKLET. They're great guys. You should see them shooting the curl. It's the ultimate. A gilt-edged guarantee for a summer of sheer happiness.

MRS. FORREST. Control yourself, Florence.

CHICKLET. *(Fiercely)* I will not control myself! I want a mother-fucking cocksucking surfborad!!!!

MRS. FORREST. I can see the effect those boys are having on you. I don't like it one bit. You will not see those boys ever again. Promise me that.

CHICKLET. I will not promise you.

MRS. FORREST. You're cold. This is what the male sex is going to do to us. It's going to tear us apart. You don't know how lucky you are being a virgin, pure and chaste.

CHICKLET. But someday I do want to marry and then I suppose I'd have to...

MRS. FORREST. Do what? Have sexual intercourse. I know how they paint it so beautifully in the movies. A man and a woman locked in embrace, soft lighting, a pitcher of Manhattans, Rachmaninoff in the background. Well, my girl, let me tell you that is not how it is. You don't know how repugnant it is having a sweaty man's thing poking at you. *(SHE jabs her finger into Chicklet)* Do you like that?

CHICKLET. Stop, you're hurting me.

MRS. FORREST. That's nothing compared to when they poke you down there.

CHICKLET. I don't believe you.

MRS. FORREST. Florence!

CHICKLET. I don't believe you. Sexual relations between a man and a woman in love is a beautiful and sacred thing. You're wrong, Mother, horribly wrong.

MRS. FORREST. The male body is coarse and ugly.

CHICKLET. Some men are beautiful.

MRS. FORREST. *(In a demonic rage)* You think men are beautiful. Well, take a look at this, Missy. *(SHE pulls from her cleavage a jock strap)* For years I've kept this, anticipating this very moment. Do you know what this is?

CHICKLET. No.

MRS. FORREST. It's a peter belt. This is the pouch that holds their swollen genitalia. Isn't this beautiful? Isn't this romantic? *(SHE slaps Chicklet with the jock strap repeatedly.)*

CHICKLET. Stop, stop.

MRS. FORREST. *(Throws the jock strap at Chicklet.)* You are a very foolish girl. And to think I spent long hours toiling over that veal scallopini. *(MRS. FORREST exits. Chicklet stares at the jock strap and whimpers.)*

CHICKLET. I'm sorry, Mommy, I'm sorry. *(Starts growling and making animal noises. In baby talk.)* She can't treat me this way. She's so mean and I'm too little to fight back ...I'm so angry...I'm so angry! I'm...I'm *(SHE bursts into demonic laughter. As ANN BOWMAN.)* I'm alive! I'm alive! Ann Bowman lives!!!!

BLACKOUT

SCENE THREE

(BERDINE is in her pajamas writing in her diary)

BERDINE. Dear Diary: Last night Chicklet showed up at my house with a real bee in her bonnet. She is determined to buy a surfboard. Her Mom said nix. Boy, parents can be grumps. Anyways, it's a good thing I won that prize money for my essay on Kierkegaard, Kant and Buber. I handed it right over. Chicklet Forrest is my best friend in the whole stratosphere. I've never told this to anyone, not even you, dear diary, but sometimes I catch her talking to herself in this weird sort of voice. I suppose some people would say she's kind of a burn-out, but you see, Chicklet is a very creative person and sometimes her imagination just sort of goes blotto but in a noodly sort of way, not a complete geek-out but just a fizzle in her research center. Sorry, that's teenage talk. Well, time to sign off, your ever faithful correspondent, Berdine.

BLACKOUT

SCENE FOUR

(The beach. YO YO and PROVOLONEY enter talking)

Yo Yo. I got my menu for the luau all made up. What do you think of marinated alligator tips? You can buy 'em frozen at Ralph's. And I thought lots of finger food, but no dips, I am so tired of dips.

PROVOLONEY. Yo Yo, would you stop with the food for

a minute.

Yo Yo. But, Provoloney, the luau is only three weeks away.

PROVOLONEY. Do you realize how much of your life is obsessed with trivia? Finger food, dips. It really upsets me how little scope you have.

Yo Yo. What are you talking about? I've got scope. *(Switching the subject)* What do you want to do with your hair for the luau?

PROVOLONEY. *(HE screams.)* See what I mean? Trivia! All this talk about receipes and hairstyles. People are gonna think you're kind of, you know, *(Makes a limp wrist)* that way.

Yo Yo. Let 'em try. I'll bash their nuts in.

PROVOLONEY. *(Trying to talk sensibly)* Yo Yo, do you ever think about the future?

Yo Yo. Yeah, that's why I'm asking you about the alligator tips.

PROVOLONEY. The far future. You're not going to be young forever. We need to plan ahead.

Yo Yo. This was such a beautiful day. You're making me so depressed.

PROVOLONEY. *(Very upbeat)* Don't be depressed, kid. Stick with me and you'll never be sorry.

(STAR CAT enters.)

STAR CAT. Hey guys, any of you seen Kanaka?

(KANAKA and CHICKLET enter.)

KANAKA. Gentlemen, the time has come for me to introduce you to the new Empress of the Seven Seas. Queen Chicklet is going to join us on the water today.

PROVOLONEY. This little twirp working our waves, give me a break.

CHICKLET. I'm not a twirp.

YO YO. Stick to the bathtub, baby, leave the Pacific to the big boys.

STAR CAT. We're too busy to be changing your diapers.

CHICKLET. You think you know everything, you stuck up prune face pickle eater.

KANAKA. You ready for a ride, Chickerino?

CHICKLET. Kanaka, these fins are ready to hit the foam. What do you say?

KANAKA. I say "Everybody, grab your surf boards and charge!" *(THEY ALL hoot and holler.)*

(LIGHTS BLACK OUT and then come BACK ON and we see CHICKLET and the BOYS riding the high waves, laughing and screaming with joy and excitement. BLACKOUT. When the LIGHTS come up THEY are carrying Chicklet on their shoulders, shouting "Hip hip hooray".)

KANAKA. What did I tell you, ain't she something else?

YO YO. *(Making a big formal bow and kissing her hand.)* I bow before the Queen Chicklet.

CHICKLET. Aw, knock it off.

PROVOLONEY. Welcome to the club. What do you say we make her our new mascot?

Yo Yo. Great.

STAR CAT. You know something, I am a stuck up prune face pickle eater. *(HE gives Chicklet a big hug and they embrace, a bit too long. EVERYONE'S CHEERS turn to OHHHHHH, and THEY are embarrassed.)* And I'll tell you what, I'll even teach you how to surf standing on your head.

CHICKLET. *(Thrilled)* You would? Really? Just the two of us?

Yo Yo. *(Imitating her)* Really? Just the two of us? *(ALL THE GUYS giggle.)*

CHICKLET. *(Embarrassed)* Well, I'd need to concentrate. I can't learn anything with you jokers around.

STAR CAT. Sure, kid, just the two of us.

PROVOLONEY. *(Acting silly)* Can we come, too?

Yo Yo. Please, please, pretty please. *(CHICKLET chases them around.)*

CHICKLET. Oh gosh, this is the way I like it, just kids, horsing around, having picnics.

PROVOLONEY. We need to give her an initiation.

STAR CAT. And how.

CHICKLET. Oh, no you don't.

PROVOLONEY. Yo Yo, give her the Chinese tickle torture.

(THEY grab her and YO YO pushes his head into her stomach ticking her with his hair, SHE screams. MARVEL ANN enters.)

MARVEL ANN. Star Cat. *(THEY drop Chicklet.)*

STAR CAT. Hey there, Marvel Ann.

STAR CAT. *(SHE wraps herself around him.)* What's all the brou-ha-ha?

KANAKA. The Chicklet turned out to be a first class surfer.

YO YO. The best.

MARVEL ANN. How marvelous for you. I wish you every...every.

CHICKLET. You should try surfing, Marvel Ann, it's great for anyone with a weight problem.

MARVEL ANN. I get my exercise indoors. Star Cat, wait til you see the dress I bought to wear to the luau. It's very...very.

CHICKLET. What, luau?

MARVEL ANN. Haven't you naughty boys told Chicklet about the luau? It's just the biggest event of the whole summer.

CHICKLET. You douche bags, why have you been holding out on me?

KANAKA. You're just not the luau type, baby.

PROVOLONEY. It's a wild night.

YO YO. Practically an orgy.

CHICKLET. I want to go.

MARVEL ANN. Besides you'll need an escort and I've already nabbed the cutest boy in town. (Flirts with an uncomfortable Star Cat. SHE strokes his hair.)

STAR CAT. Ow, you're pulling my hair.

MARVEL ANN. You promised you'd go to the pier with me today. I'm in the mood for a nice big banana split. Doesn't that sound tasty?

STAR CAT. Very, very. See you guys later. (THEY exit.)

CHICKLET. You all think you're real clever not telling me about the luau but I'm going and I'm going to make a splash like you've never seen.

(The incredibly glamourous movie star, BETTINA BARNES, enters in a big hat and dark glasses. THE BOYS stare at her transfixed as SHE unfolds her blanket and sits on the beach.)

Yo Yo. Zowie!

PROVOLONEY. Hot dog!

KANAKA. Let's check out her I.D. *(THEY approach her.)*

CHICKLET. Hey guys, don't bother with her.

KANAKA. *(To Bettina)* And then the Papa Bear said "Who's been sleeping in my sandbox?"

BETTINA. *(Surprised, lowers her sunglasses)* Pardon me?

KANAKA. What brings you here to grace our turf?

BETTINA. *(Breathily innocent)* Am I trespassing? I had no idea.

PROVOLONEY. You look real familiar. Do you know Lenny Pinkowitz?

BETTINA. *(Alarmed)* Is he a shutterbug?

CHICKLET. Hey guys, come on.

Yo Yo. Can we ask you your name?

BETTINA. I'm afraid I can't answer that.

CHICKLET. Are you incognito?

BETTINA. *(Not comprehending)* No, I'm German-Irish.

KANAKA. Are there people after you?

BETTINA. I have a whole motion picture studio after me and the entire press corp. Haven't you read the newspapers? I'm Bettina Barnes. *(Gasps)* I shouldn't have told you.

CHICKLET. Bettina Barnes, the movie star.

BETTINA. Actress.

CHICKLET. You disappeared from the set of your new movie. The police think you've been kidnapped.

BETTINA. I was never kidnapped. I ran away.

PROVOLONEY. Why would you run away from a movie?

BETTINA. You don't know what it's like being exploited by those lousy flesh peddlers and power brokers. Everyone wanting a little piece. I'm not a pepperoni.

KANAKA. I saw you in that movie "Sex Kittens Go To Outer Space."

BETTINA. That was a good film. The director had a vision but then I had to do the four sequels. Quel trash. I couldn't go on. They have no respect for the rights of the individual.

YO YO. We'll respect you.

BETTINA. *(Touched)* Would you really? Isn't that what all human beings desire, respect? That's why I'm on the lam, to get me some.

CHICKLET. Where are you going to go?

BETTINA. New York. I've been accepted to study with Lee Strasberg. But first I thought I'd hide out here to get some rest and relaxation. I've rented that beach house over there. I signed the lease under my real name Frieda Deefendorfer. You won't squeal on me, will you? *(THE BOYS all promise they won't.)* You're so sweet. You can be kind of like my brothers. *(To Chicklet)* And you, you're perky. With a new hairstyle and the right makeup, you could be almost pretty.

(BERDINE enters.)

BERDINE. Chicklet! There you are. I thought I'd find you here. You were supposed to meet me at the malt shop. I was waiting there over an hour when... *(SHE sees BETTINA and screams.)* Bettina Barnes! *(THE BOYS grab her and hold her mouth closed.)*

CHICKLET. She's incognito.

BERDINE. Bettina Barnes. In person. You have the most beautiful eyelashes I'ves ever seen on any mammal.

BETTINA. You're very kind.

BERDINE. I loved you in "The Pizza Waitress with Three Heads." You were so real. When they trapped you on top of the Pizzeria, you made me feel what it's like to have three heads and be shot in each one of them.

BETTINA. *(Intensely)* Did I really?

BERDINE. Oh yes, Miss Barnes.

BETTINA. *(Tenderly)* Call me Miss B. I know I could be a great actress if I found the right vehicle.

PROVOLONEY. She needs wheels.

YO YO. The lady needs wheels.

KANAKA. We'll get you a car.

BERDINE. No, she means she needs a great role that will reveal the many facets of her kaleidoscopic persona.

BETTINA. *(Confused)* What did she say?

BERDINE. Sometimes even the great don't understand their own power. You are more than a mere sex kitten. You are the feminine embodiment of the nietzschian superman. Ever striving, striking a blow for the truth in the eternal battle of the sexes. Onward, Bettina! "And whatever will break on our truths, let it break! Many a house hath yet to be built". Thus spake Zarathustra.

BETTINA. That's what I've been telling my agents for

months. You're smart. What's your name?

BERDINE. Berdine.

BETTINA. I desperately need a secretary slash companion slash masseuse. How would you like a job for the summer?

BERDINE. I don't know, Miss B. I've got a big reading list to get through. And I'm still not finished with "The Idiot."

BETTINA. *(With great sympathy)* You've got man trouble?

PROVOLONEY. Hey guys, let's invite Miss Barnes to the luau.

BERDINE. What luau?

KANAKA. The first full moon of the summer, we have a luau slash barbecue. It's a night no one ever forgets.

BERDINE. *(Sarcastically)* Gee, thanks Chicklet for inviting me.

CHICKLET. I just heard about it.

BERDINE. Like hey I really believe that.

CHICKLET. It's the truth.

BERDINE. The truth is that we're not connecting at all anymore.

CHICKLET. What are you talking about?

BERDINE. Let me spell it out for you then. In the past few weeks, you never return my phone calls, you've cancelled out of the last five times we're supposed to get together and today you stood me up at Augie's malt shop. I don't think you want to be best friends anymore.

CHICKLET. I'm sorry, I just...

BERDINE. *(Holding back tears)* Everyone said we were too close. I never thought this could happen. Not to us.

BETTINA. Please don't argue on my account.

CHICKLET. Don't cry. Look, let's talk about this in private. How about meeting me at Augie's tomorrow.

BERDINE. So you can stand me up again? No, thank you. Chicklet, my closing remarks to you are these. I hope you enjoy all your new hipster friends cause you just lost your best and oldest one. Miss Barnes, I've reconsidered and I'd love to be your secretary. When do I start?

BETTINA. Pronto. We're going to have a great time. *(Takes her arm)* I'm going to let you in on all my innermost secrets. Let's go back to my bungalow and have lunch. You do know how to make Crab Louis, don't you?

BERDINE. I don't think so.

BETTINA. No sweat. We'll have peanut butter and jelly... *(As an afterthought)* on toast points.

PROVOLONEY. Think about the luau.

KANAKA. Think about me.

BETTINA. *(Seductively)* How could I forget you.

YO YO. *(Extends his hand to Bettina to shake hands.)* It's been great meeting you.

BETTINA. *(SHE turns to Yo Yo and takes his hand.)* My, what great big hands you have.

YO YO. *(Leering)* You know what they say about big hands and big feet.

BETTINA. *(Studying his hand intently)* Yes, most interesting.

CHICKLET. Are you a palmist or something?

BETTINA. No, nothing like that. I just have these incredible instincts about people. I seem to know how they tick.

YO YO. So what do you see?

BETTINA. I bet you're very good with hair.

Yo Yo. You mean running my fingers through it.

BETTINA. No, I mean setting it.

Yo Yo. *(Upset at the suggestion he's a fag.)* Hey, wait just a minute...

BETTINA. *(Very soothing and gentle)* That's nothing to be ashamed of. It's a special gift. *(The OTHER GUYS snicker.)* I've got a slew of wigs with me. Let's go to my bungalow, lock the door and play beauty salon.

PROVOLONEY. *(Acting sexy)* Can I come too? I'd love to lock the door and play with you.

BETTINA. Hey, Berdine, as a great philosopher once said "the more the merrier." Let's go!

Yo Yo. Yeah, go, go, go. *(BETTINA exits followed by Yo Yo, PROVOLONEY and BERDINE. KANAKA pulls Chicklet back.)*

KANAKA. Hey, Chicklet.

CHICKLET. Don't you want to go to Bettina's?

KANAKA. Nah, it's kids stuff to be impressed with her. *(Checks to see if they are alone.)*

CHICKLET. Who are you looking for?

KANAKA. I want to make sure we're alone. Uh, it's Yo Yo's birthday coming up and...

CHICKLET. I thought he said it was...

KANAKA. No, it's real soon and I thought you could help me make him a present.

CHICKLET. Like what?

KANAKA. A kite. He's flipped over kites. What do you think of that?

CHICKLET. A kite. That's okay.

KANAKA. Kites. He becomes like a different person

when he's flying a kite.

CHICKLET. I never made one before but...

KANAKA. *(To himself)* What were we talking about? Do you see that fish jumping out of the water?

CHICKLET. No, where?

KANAKA. I'm crazy for fish, aren't you?

CHICKLET. *(Shrugs)* Feh. Kanaka, are you all right?

KANAKA. *(Giving up)* No, I must be out of my mind. Forget it. Geez, I'm embarrassed. Is my face red? *(When CHICKLET hears red she laughs wildly and turns into ANN BOWMAN.)*

KANAKA. *(Elated)* It was a red kite!

CHICKLET. *(As ANN BOWMAN)* It most certainly was, darling. As red as your ass when I finish spanking you.

KANAKA. Oh yes, Mistress Ann. I've been a bad boy. I need a spanking.

CHICKLET. I've got you under my spell. You would do anything I asked. *(SHE turns into TYLENE, a black checkout girl.)* But if she asked me to work overtime at that Safeway, she be out of her mind.

KANAKA. Ann?

CHICKLET. Who you be calling Ann, my name is Tylene. Tylene Carmichael Carmel.

KANAKA. What?

CHICKLET. I be working at the checkout, it goin' on four-thirty and I'm fixin' to leave. My boyfriend, he's taking me to see Chubby Checker.

KANAKA. Ann, come back, Ann, are you there?

CHICKLET. Would you let me finish? What I am saying is my supervisor, Miss Feeley, she asks me to work overtime. She thinks she so cool, she...

KANAKA. *(Shakes her)* Stop it. Bring Ann back!

CHICKLET. *(Indicates a switchblade's in her pocket.)* Back off! I cut you. I cut you. I got me a blade. I cut you.

KANAKA. *(Terrified)* That's cool. That's cool.

CHICKLET. No way no white son of a bitch be grabbin at me. No way, no way... *(Returns as ANN)* No way you can escape my domination. The world has tried to suppress me, to deny my very existence but I have risen like a phoenix to claim my birthright.

KANAKA. What's that?

CHICKLET. World domination. Ann Bowman, Dominatrix Empress of the planet Earth. Has a catchy ring, don't you think?

KANAKA. Yes, Mistress Ann.

CHICKLET. I wonder if your little friends might make excellent slaves. We must catch them in butterfly nets and put them in cages. Once their spirit is broken, they shall learn to serve their Mistress Ann.

KANAKA. Cages. But won't they suspect you're up to no good?

CHICKLET. I am not only a first class general. I am also a brilliant actress. I will pose as dear little Chicklet and infiltrate the teen set.

KANAKA. Look, I think I've gotten in over my head. I can't do something like this.

CHICKLET. *(Grabs him)* You deny me! No one denies me, darling. You need what only I can offer. Face it, you're weak, you're a pushover for me. You sing to the coppers and I'll finger you as the fall guy. You made me lose my temper. It's time for fun and games. Shall we proceed to your place? Kanaka, move it! *(SHE throws her head back and laughs. THEY exit.)*

BLACKOUT

SCENE FIVE

The Beach. PROVOLONEY and YO YO enter.

YO YO. I don't know, Provoloney, it sounds too easy.

PROVOLONEY. I tell you, the ideas that make millions are deceptively simple. Bettina Barnes is on the lookout for a movie that will win her an Oscar. We've got to find it for her.

YO YO. But that means writing and I'm not so good with sentences.

PROVOLONEY. In Hollywood, only flunkies do any writing. The smart guys write treatments. The studio pays big money just for ideas. We come up with a great notion for a flick and we can rake in the moola without putting in a comma.

YO YO. You have any ideas?

PROVOLONEY. My brain's bursting with them. Westerns, sci-fi, musicals.

YO YO. Well, I think...

PROVOLONEY. Quiet on the set. I need inspiration. I

need a concept.

Yo Yo. I think Bettina should play the richest woman in the world.

PROVOLONEY. *(His eyes closed)* Yeah, my mind's working now. Go on.

Yo Yo. Her old man wants her to marry this prince but he's kind of a drip so she ankles out of Philly and heads westward to Malibu.

PROVOLONEY. It's all coming to me. I'm cookin'. Go on.

Yo Yo. She's got so much cash that she buys the whole beach. There's this real hot surf bum who lives there and he don't like the idea of being evicted. They decide to smoke the peace pipe and the stud offers to teach her to scuba dive.

PROVOLONEY. This is great. I can see the whole thing. A billboard fifty feet high. Bettina Barnes in a wet suit.

Yo Yo. I see this real big scene when they first dive underwater. *(YO YO mimes going underwater.)*

PROVOLONEY. *(HE dives too.)* They swim past picturesque coral reefs and dolphins.

Yo Yo. And they bump into each other. *(THEY mime all the next activity.)*

PROVOLONEY. And they get their feet caught in some seaweed...and their bodies are locked into each other.

Yo Yo. They can't get out?

PROVOLONEY. *(Transfixed)* Uh uh. Their eyes meet. Every night he's dreamt of her long flowing hair, her ivory skin, her biceps.

Yo Yo. She feels powerless to resist his raw brute strength. Is this where they kiss for the first time?

PROVOLONEY. They've always wanted to but they were too scared.

Yo Yo. I guess underwater it doesn't matter much.

PROVOLONEY. I guess not.

(THEY slowly kiss. CANNONS go off. BELLS ring. The 1812 Overture is played. THEY break apart.)

PROVOLONEY. *(Scared)* Uh, Yo Yo, I better write this down before I forget it.

Yo Yo. *(Thrilled)* I won't forget it.

PROVOLONEY. *(Embarrassed and remorseful)* I met this lady who works in the library. She said she'd teach me how to use her typewriter.

Yo Yo. That's good.

PROVOLONEY. Yeah. Maybe afterwards, I'll...I'll ball her. *(PROVOLONEY exits.)*

BLACKOUT

SCENE SIX

The beach beyond Bettina's house. BERDINE is writing in her diary.

BERDINE. Dear Diary: Gear up for another helping of Berdine's flaming self pity. I miss Chicklet so much. Ever since she got that darn surf board, nothing's been the same. I wish I'd never given her that money. A girl's best friend is something very special. And Chicklet's more than just my best friend. It's like we're one person. I know that sounds kooky but it's true. Oh, life is but a meaningless charade, death the ultimate absurdity. I am living proof of Sartre's existential concept of nausea. Gosh, I wish I had a Tums. Of course, I've been very busy working for Miss Barnes. She's a nice lady but very complicated.

(BETTINA enters stretching.)

BERDINE. Good morning, Miss B!

BETTINA. What a splendiforous morning. I can't tell you how grand it feels to be away from that salacious Hollywood rat race. I was so tense. You can't imagine the hubbub in my lower lumbar region.

BERDINE. Well, this week has done wonders for you. You look like a completely different person.

BETTINA. *(Suspicious and paranoid)* Who? What's her measurements?

BERDINE. No, what I meant was...oh... *(Sees telegram in her hand)* Oh! Miss Barnes, that telegram arrived that you were waiting for.

BETTINA. *(Excited)* Oh wow, I'm scared to open it. It's from the studio. I've asked them to release me from my contract. *(Opens it)* I'm too scared to read it. It's awful being this vulnerable. *(To Berdine)* You read it to me.

BERDINE. *(Reading)* Dear Bettina, up yours, stop, with turpentine, stop. New picture "Sex Kittens Go Bossa

Nova" starts lensing September first. Be there or expect legal action. Stop. Love Sid Rosen. *(Stops reading)* Oh Bettina, I'm so sorry. You poor little thing.

BETTINA. *(Tough as nails and in a low rough voice)* That cheap son of a bitch can't do this to me. He slaps me with a subpoena and I'll have his balls on a plate.

BERDINE. *(Shocked)* Bettina.

BETTINA. *(Pacing furious)* After all the money I made for those bastards. They can't do this to me. I'm Bettina Barnes. I'm no flash in the pan that'll take any piece of crap. I'm playing hard ball, baby.

BERDINE. Have you read the script? Maybe it's not bad.

BETTINA. Not bad! Lassie could fart out a better script.

(YO YO and PROVOLONEY enter. PROVOLONEY is tricked up in his notion of a hollywood movie mogul.)

PROVOLONEY. Hey there, Miss Barnes, I hear you got some work you'd like us to do.

BETTINA. *(Soft and vulnerable)* Oh, yeah, something. I needed something done. I'm so forgetful. *(Remembers)* Oh, yes. Last night I was sleepwalking and I suddenly woke up and discovered this adorable little garden in my back yard. During the last storm, all the little trees and shrubbery must have broken and it's a dreadful mess. Could you clear it up for me? And then we can have swell parties. I make delicious jalapeno pancakes.

YO YO. Sure thing. We'll clean it up.

PROVOLONEY. *(Nervously)* Excuse me Miss Barnes, do

you think I could talk to you for a moment?

BETTINA. But of course.

PROVOLONEY. *(With an air of bravado)* I never told you this before but this surf bum business is just a facade, I'm really a screenwriter.

BERDINE. You're what?

YO YO. He's a screenwriter.

PROVOLONEY. Written tons of stuff, TV, radio. I've got a development deal going for me at Columbia. Meeting you yesterday gave me the inspiration for a new picture. A big picture, cinemascope, 3-D, smell-o-vision.

BETTINA. *(Touched)* Really, I inspired you?

PROVOLONEY. You certainly did. It's just a treatment, really, an idea.

YO YO. But it's a great one.

BETTINA. I love a man with a big idea.

PROVOLONEY. Columbia's been putting the screws on me to make it with Kim.

BETTINA. *(Very impressed)* You know Kim Novak?

PROVOLONEY. Great gal but dead eyes, blank, an empty screen. This idea...

BETTINA. Oh, tell me all about it.

PROVOLONEY. The setting: Malibu Beach. I see you as the daughter of a shipping tycoon. You...

BERDINE. ...leave finishing school and meet a handsome surf bum who teaches you how to scuba dive. "The Girl From Rock n' Roll Beach," Starring Mamie Van Doren, Allied Artists, 1960, Albert Zugsmith, Producer.

PROVOLONEY. Yeah, well, it's a lot like that, only better. You can have the hole megillah for two thousand dollars.

BETTINA. Two thousand dollars. It sounds most intriguing but I think for my first independent feature, I should play a typical girl of today, someone who the audience can identify with and yet a girl with a personal problem, like psoriasis. However, maybe we can develop this further.

PROVOLONEY. Bettina baby, I don't want to pressure you but...

BETTINA. *(Looks offstage)* Oh, look, there's your little friend, Chicklet. I don't know, there's something kind of funny about her.

(CHICKLET enters with a wild red feather boa, and smoking out of a long cigarette holder.)

CHICKLET. *(In ANN BOWMAN'S voice)* Berdine darling! It's been eons since we last met.

BERDINE. *(Shocked)* Chicklet?

CHICKLET. Miss Barnes, a delight as always. *(To the boys)* Hello, boys. *(THEY ALL say "Hi" in a dazed manner.)* I do hope these boys have been showing you a good time. They taught me how to surf and now I'm positively addicted to shooting the curl, as they say.

BETTINA. They're helping me fix up my backyard.

CHICKLET. How utterly fab. Boys, I have a little job for you.

YO YO. Chicklet, are you feeling all right?

CHICKLET. Just swellsville. I'd like to have a cage built.

PROVOLONEY. A bird cage?

CHICKLET. No, something suitable for a bigger animal, or animals.

BERDINE. Chicklet, what are you talking about?

CHICKLET. *(Becomes herself)* Berdine. Where am I? *(Sees the boa and cigarette holder)* What's all this?

BERDINE. You tell me.

CHICKLET. *(At a loss)* Ohhh, I found it in the garbage outside the Club Transvestite. *(SHE laughs hysterically but no one else does.)* Eek.

PROVOLONEY. You wanted us to build you a cage.

CHICKLET. A cage? Don't be a doofus...Anyways, now that I am here...Berdine, I feel awful for the way I've been treating you. I don't know what could possess me being so rude like that. You should just belt me. Go on and belt me.

BERDINE. I couldn't.

CHICKLET. Really. You're like my...How do I...

BERDINE. I know. You are too.

CHICKLET. But more than that. We've always...

BERDINE. That's true. But still sometimes...

CHICKLET. Oh, but we...

BERDINE. Yeah, but I wouldn't want...

CHICKLET. You don't really want...

BERDINE. I just don't...

CHICKLET. Trust me. C'mon. Please Berdine, please go on being my best friend for a zillion more years. What do you say?

BERDINE. For a zillion trillion more years. To infinity. *(THEY hug.)*

CHICKLET. Will you be my escort to the luau?

BERDINE. You don't think I'm too much of a nerd-brain?

CHICKLET. Of course not.

PROVOLONEY. What are you two going to do for the talent show?

CHICKLET. What talent show?

YO YO. That's part of the tradition. Everyone's gotta get up and do an act. I'm doing my Jane Russell imitation. *(Pulls his shirt out like bosoms)* Boom titty boom.

BERDINE. I know. Remember that act we did for the Kiwanis Club Variety Night? The costume is in my attic.

CHICKLET. You got yourself a partner. *(THEY shake)*

BETTINA. I'm glad you patched things up. I'm so in awe of friendship. I mean, never having any. We better get started on the garden before it gets dark. Come on, kids. *(ALL THE KIDS including CHICKLET and BERDINE exit laughing and singing.)*

(STAR CAT and MARVEL ANN stroll on)

MARVEL ANN. Star Cat, you mean little devil, I was up all night thinking about you.

STAR CAT. *(Excited)* You were?

MARVEL ANN. Uh huh. Couldn't sleep a wink. You wanna know what I was thinking?

STAR CAT. Empty that beautiful head of yours.

MARVEL ANN. I was thinking that you and I are going to be united as one forever.

STAR CAT. *(Nervously)* Gee, Marvel Ann, are you sure I'm good enough for you? I wouldn't want you to settle.

MARVEL ANN. Settle? You're the dreamboat of all time, generous, always thinking of others, sensitive.

STAR CAT. Aw, I'm just a good for nothing surf bum.

MARVEL ANN. That's not true. You're just riddled with greatness. I look in your eyes and honestly, I see dollar signs.

STAR CAT. You don't understand. I'm rejecting those false values. I refuse to worship the golden calf.

MARVEL ANN. *(Petulant but still pleasant)* You don't know what you want. I think it's a horrid shame that you're throwing away a great future as a psychiatrist. All your wonderful compassion going to waste. *(STAR CAT tries to interject)* Oh, I know what you're going to say, "I just want a little shack by the water." Well, you can't expect me to live like that. Imagine me serving my friends Steak Diane Flambe in a lean-to. *(STAR CAT tries to interject)* Don't say a word, I know what you're thinking, "Marvel Ann is such a lovely person, in time she'd grow used to such a life." *(With growing emotion and intensity)* Well, I'd be humiliated. Oh, I can read you like the funny papers. *(With growing fury)* You think I'm so head over heels in love with you, I'll accept whatever crumbs you have to offer. Well, no siree Bob, I am hardly a desperate female. Ohhh, look at that awful expression in your eyes. I bet you think you don't even have to marry me, that I'd shack up with you like a common whore. Now you've really done it. I am livid. How could you think of such filth! You are a selfish, egocentric creep and my advice to you is to straighten up, buckle down and apply yourself like any other decent, normal Presbyterian!! *(SHE stalks off in a fury)*

(CHICKLET enters.)

STAR CAT. *(Angrily)* Hey, what are you doing here?

CHICKLET. I didn't know you owned this beach. I don't see your initials carved into the ocean.

STAR CAT. Sorry. I didn't mean to bark at you.

CHICKLET. *(Sympathetically)* Girl trouble?

STAR CAT. Yeah, that dame wants to put a ball and chain around my neck.

CHICKLET. Well, don't you dare let her. I think it's swell the way you guys live.

STAR CAT. You do?

CHICKLET. Sure. Flying about as free as a gull, never having a care in the world.

STAR CAT. You're on my beam. Marvel Ann doesn't understand me at all. She thinks she can see through me like wax paper but she's wrong. I'm an extremely complex person with deep rooted neuroses and anxieties. You wouldn't understand that, you're just a kid.

CHICKLET. *(Offended)* I am not just a kid. I'm capable of intensely passionate adult feelings. If you didn't have so much sea foam in your eyes, you'd notice I'm a budding young woman.

STAR CAT. *(Amused)* Honey, your buds have a long way to bloom.

CHICKLET. Evidently some people don't share that opinion.

STAR CAT. Like who?

CHICKLET. Oh, some people.

STAR CAT. Like nobody.

CHICKLET. Like Kanaka. He thinks I'm, how did he put it? I'm a luscious voluptuary.

STAR CAT. Liar. I know Kanaka. He could have any dame in Malibu.

CHICKLET. Well, he wants me.

STAR CAT. How do you know?

CHICKLET. It's one of those mystical things a woman feels instinctively in her soul.

STAR CAT. Get over it.

CHICKLET. *(Defensively)* He taught me how to surf, didn't he? And he tries to see me every day and he always makes sure we're completely alone. As a matter of fact, I'm headed over to Kanaka's shack right now, for an extremely intimate tête-a-tête.

STAR CAT. I don't believe it.

CHICKLET. *Chacon á son gout.* That means, each to his own, you dope. He thinks I'm special.

STAR CAT. I think you're trying to make me jealous. What a screwy kid you are. I bet you've got a great big fat crush on me.

CHICKLET. *(Blushing)* You've got a great big fat ego.

STAR CAT. Hey c'mon, let's call it a truce. I like you, kid. I do. And I think you're very special.

CHICKLET. Please don't patronize me.

STAR CAT. *(Turns her around and hold her chin)* You are special.

CHICKLET. *(Vulnerable)* I am?

STAR CAT. And cute.

CHICKLET. I am?

STAR CAT. You need somebody to protect you.

CHICKLET. Protect me from what?

STAR CAT. *(Friendly)* Oh, from big bad wolves. You could be a tasty morsel, to some wolf.

CHICKLET. What about to you?

STAR CAT. I suppose I could be dangerously tempted.

CHICKLET. Oh, Star Cat.

(STAR CAT opens his mouth to sing. We hear an obviously dubbed recording of a teen idol singing the "Chicklet Theme Song." Suddenly, the record gets stuck, and we hear the needle scratch across the record. There is an uncomfortable silence.)

STAR CAT. I guess I'll have to tell you how I feel. You're a one of a kind girl, Chicklet, like no one I've ever met.

CHICKLET. What about Marvel Ann? Is she one of a kind too?

STAR CAT. *(Smiles, embarrassed)* Well...

CHICKLET. Star Cat, what do boys do when they're alone with a girl?

STAR CAT. You can't ask me such a question.

CHICKLET. Why not? I want to know.

STAR CAT. They neck. I don't know.

CHICKLET. What do you do with Marvel Ann?

STAR CAT. This is embarrassing, Chicklet.

CHICKLET. Tell me.

(Romantic music sneaks in through the end of the scene.)

STAR CAT. She nestles real close to me.

CHICKLET. *(Cuddles next to him)* Kind of like this?

STAR CAT. *(Horny and nervous)* Yeah, sort of like that. I hold her in my arms. And she holds me back.

CHICKLET. Like this? And then what do you do?

STAR CAT. I kiss the back of her neck. I can't do this with you.

CHICKLET. Pretend I'm Marvel Ann. I need to know this sort of thing. For my own protection.

STAR CAT. I stroke her arm and she kisses my chest. *(CHICKLET kisses his chest)* And we can feel our hearts beating as one. We find ourselves swaying to the same personal rhythm.

CHICKLET. You takes you clothes off, right?

STAR CAT. *(Lost in the moment)* Uh huh.

CHICKLET. You got your clothes off. Then what?

STAR CAT. I caress her smooth satiny flesh. It glistens in the moonlight. She gently touches my muscles with her fingertips. Our bodies seem to float to the ground. We're entwined. And then I slowly slide my penis into her vagina. Simultaneously, she licks her index finger and inserts it up my rectum as I pump my penis...

(During this last graphic part, CHICKLET is horrified and at the end of his speech, SHE screams as if in a horror movie and runs away.)

STAR CAT. *(Shouting after her)* Chicklet, come back!

BLACKOUT

SCENE SEVEN

Kanaka's shack. STAR CAT enters.

STAR CAT. Kanaka, where are you? You home?

(KANAKA enters)

KANAKA. Hey pal, what are you doing in my shack without an invite? I don't dig surprise visits.

STAR CAT. I'm looking for Chicklet.

KANAKA. She's not here, not yet.

STAR CAT. But she will be.

KANAKA. Yeah, and what's it to you? She's not your chick.

STAR CAT. And she shouldn't be yours either. She's only a kid.

KANAKA. That's all you know.

STAR CAT. If you've laid a finger on her...

KANAKA. Hey, cool out. You don't know the score. There is more to that Chicklet than meets the old eyeball. There's like two Chicklets in one, man.

STAR CAT. What are you talking about?

KANAKA. It's wild. She's like twins in one bod. One's an angel and the other's a she devil. She calls herself Ann Bowman and she's like a demon. And the weird thing is, I can turn her off and on like a flashlight.

STAR CAT. You're talking crazy.

58

KANAKA. *(Desperate)* Can I trust you, buddy? Will you swear by the code of the King of the Sea you won't tell anyone any of this?

STAR CAT. Yeah, I swear.

KANAKA. I got it heavy for Ann Bowman. She's like a drug running through my veins and I can't shake her. I'm even gonna let her shave me, man.

STAR CAT. You're not making any sense.

KANAKA. Nothing makes sense. But I need her. I need Mistress Ann.

STAR CAT. Get a hold of yourself.

KANAKA. She's power mad. She's plotting to take over the world. First Malibu and then Sacramento. She wants to set up concentration camps for her enemies and public executions and her own NBC variety series.

(CHICKLET enters unseen by them)

STAR CAT. If this is true, you've got to stop this!

KANAKA. I can't give her up. I'd kill for Ann Bowman.

CHICKLET. Who's Ann Bowman?

STAR CAT. Stay out of this.

KANAKA. Star Cat, I want you to meet a friend of mine. Hey, Chicklet, you remember that kite we saw, that...

STAR CAT. You son of a... *(STAR CAT tries to punch out Kanaka. THEY fight. CHICKLET tries to get between them. Suddenly THEY ALL start to move in slow motion and we see Chicklet get in the way of STAR CAT'S punch and slowly drift to the floor.)* Chicklet, are you all right?

KANAKA. Now you've done it, man. *(THEY BOTH hold her as SHE comes to)*

CHICKLET. What happened? Where am I?
KANAKA. In my beach shack.

(There's WILD KNOCKING at the door)

KANAKA. The door's open.

(MRS. FORREST enters in a furious state)

MRS. FORREST. Well, this is a pretty sight, I must say.
KANAKA. Who the hell are you?
CHICKLET. Mom, what are you doing here?
MRS. FORREST. Young lady, you are in big trouble.
STAR CAT. Mrs. Forrest, you don't understand.
MRS. FORREST. Indeed I do understand. I also know the penalty for seducing a minor. You and your buddy will be sitting in stir for quite a while.
CHICKLET. Mother, would you stop. Kanaka and Star Cat are my friends. There was nothing dirty involved.
MRS. FORREST. How dare you speak to me in that manner. I see now clearly the effect of a permissive childhood. All the gentle caring, the indulgences, the little treats. How wrong I was. Life will be quite different from now on. I am going to mete out a severe punishment for you, young lady, most severe indeed.
CHICKLET. Mother.
MRS. FORREST. Get in the car. *(CHICKLET exits. To the boys.)* You two scum bags had better get yourselves a good mouthpiece, cause I'm gonna tear your peckers off in that courtroom. Good evening, gentlemen.

BLACKOUT

SCENE EIGHT

BERDINE is in her bedroom writing in her diary.

BERDINE. Dear Diary: This entry is strictly confidential. Chicklet's Mom is on the warpath. She locked the Chicklet in her room and has refused her all visitors, yours truly included. Panicsville, here I come. The luau is tomorrow night! Chicklet and I simply have to be there. We've been rehearsing our Siamese twin act all week. It's gonna be the greatest thing ever. I swear, grownups think they can run the whole world. Like Nathan Hale or Lafayette Escadrille, there is only one person who refuses to bow down before tyranny, I Berdine! I'm marching over to Chicklet's right now and get her out of there. I defy you stars, nothing and I mean nothing is going to stop us from going to the luau.

BLACKOUT

(Chicklet's bedroom. CHICKLET is bound and gagged. A T.V. tray with dinner is placed before her. MRS. FORREST enters with creepy serenity.)

MRS. FORREST. What a dinner. I'm so stuffed I can hardly move. I certainly enjoyed my T-bone steak, so bloody rare and juicy. *(Thoughtfully)* I may have overcooked the lima beans. Vegetables are delicate creatures. *(With*

vulnerable charm) Still, I have to admit, it was delicious.
(Still lovely) This meal could have been yours, Chicklet, if
you hadn't chosen to disobey me. Do you finally see what
I mean about making the right choices in life? It's a
rough world, darling, with a lot of crummy people out
there. You can't be impressed with them. *(With force)*
Believe me, they stink! *(Back to her charming manner)* I'm
afraid I still see defiance in your eyes. You have so much
to learn. *(SHE touches the gag restraint. Jokes.)* I bet you think
I've taken this gag too far. *(Laughs at her joke)* That's funny.
(SHE gives the gag a tighter tug) I think we'll keep this on a
wee bit longer. *(SHE exits)*

*(BERDINE enters swinging in through the window on a rope
made of bedsheets)*

BERDINE. Chicklet! What has she done to you? *(SHE
tries to untie her)* You poor helpless thing. How did she do
this? These must be army knots. Don't be mad but I
think our top priority should be your arms. I hope this
experience won't make you bitter and pessimistic. Just
hold on. I'm not saying you should be a grinning idiot
but as Schopenhauer says "we should strive for a tragic
optimism." *(CHICKLET grunts)* It's not easy, the greater
the intelligence, the greater the capacity for suffering.
(CHICKLET grunts)

*(MRS. FORREST enters unbeknownst to Berdine whose back is to
her. CHICKLET sees Mrs. Forrest and grunts trying to warn
Berdine.)*

BERDINE. I can't get it. We'll have to get you out of here the way you are. Give a little hop. *(BERDINE turns around and sees Mrs. Forrest)*

MRS. FORREST. *(Excluding charm)* Hello Berdine. How kind of you to visit us. I've made a terrific bunt cake. Care for a slice?

BERDINE. *(Totally freaked)* That's okay. My Mom made butterscotch pudding for dessert. I've really got to get along.

MRS. FORREST. Such a pity. I was hoping you'd watch "Bonanza" with us. Are you planning to take Chicklet with you?

BERDINE. Uh yes, actually. We've been rehearsing...I mean we've been working on a science project together. Mendel's theory of propagation and all that stuff.

MRS. FORREST. I'm afraid Mendel will have to propagate without the help of my Chicklet. She's been a naughty girl and naughtiness must be punished. Chicklet lied to me and more importantly she lied to herself. Berdine, you must be brutally honest with yourself, cruelly honest. Rip away the cobwebs of delusion. Dig and find the ugliness at the base of your soul, expose it to the light, examine it, let it wither, then kill it!!! Girl, know thyself! *(Trying to control her emotions)* It's the only way.

BERDINE. *(Caught up in the debate and forgetting Chicklet)* Mrs. Forrest, I fervently disagree. *(CHICKLET grunts desperately)* One must seek self knowledge but illusion is necessary to preserve a sense of innocence.

MRS. FORREST. *(Pulls Chicklet to her)* None are innocent, all are guilty.

BERDINE. *(Realizes Mrs. Forrest isn't on her wave-length)*

Mrs. Forrest, you're a fascinating conversationalist but I've really got to get Chicklet out of here.

MRS. FORREST. *(Forcefully)* Chicklet is grounded!

BERDINE. Get out of my way, Mrs. Forrest. I am rescuing Chicklet. You are not responsible for your actions.

MRS. FORREST. You take one more step and you'll be a nerd with no teeth.

BERDINE. To save Chicklet, I would gladly wear a complete bridge. *(BERDINE moves and MRS. FORREST grabs her. THEY wrestle to the ground and fight it out. Finally BERDINE gets the upper hand and sits on Mrs. Forrest's chest, pinning her down.)* Chicklet, run for it!

MRS. FORREST. *(Gasping)* Get off me! You big cow. *(CHICKLET with her feet bound slowly hops offstage while BERDINE talks to Mrs. Forrest)*

BERDINE. *(Ties Mrs. Forrest up with bedsheets)* I'm really sorry, Mrs. Forrest, for being so disrespectful. This is highly uncharacteristic behavior for me but you know, lately I've been cramming myself with Sartrean existentialism so maybe I'm unduly influenced by his committment to extreme action. Gosh, this is deep.

BLACKOUT

SCENE NINE

The luau. LIGHTS up and PROVOLONEY, YO YO, KANAKA,

BETTINA, NICKY and DEE DEE are all having a wild time. STAR CAT enters.

STAR CAT. Marvel Ann, Marvel Ann! Has anybody seen Marvel Ann?

EVERYONE. No!

NICKY. Hey cats, let's Limbo!

(THEY do a big limbo number and hoot it up. At the height of the festivities MARVEL ANN enters, her hair half shaved off. BETTINA is the first to see her and screams.)

MARVEL ANN. *(Hysterical)* My hair! My hair! I'm gonna kill the bastard who did this.

STAR CAT. Marvel Ann, what happened?

MARVEL ANN. I was lying on the beach with my eyes closed. Someone knocked me out. I woke up and the bastard was shaving my head. They'd already shaved my beaver.

PROVOLONEY. Couldn't you see who it was?

MARVEL ANN. No, they had glued stripper's pasties over my eyes. I'm so humiliated.

KANAKA. *(In terror to STAR CAT)* Ann Bowman strikes again.

BETTINA. Honey, in a few months you'll have a cute pixie. *(MARVEL ANN groans. PROVOLONEY jumps up trying to get everyone's attention.)*

PROVOLONEY. Quiet, everybody. QUIET! *(EVERYONE settles down to watch the show)* Good evening and welcome to Provoloney's Pacific Follies. How is everybody out there? Ready for a great show? Let me hear you.

NICKY. Boo! Get on with the show. *(EVERYONE joins in booing)*

PROVOLONEY. I love these audiences, the greatest in the world. I tell you, coming over here tonight I couldn't help but be reminded of the story of the Stewardess in from Cleveland. She arrives at...

NICKY. We heard that already. Bring on the girls. *(EVERYONE joins in)*

PROVOLONEY. Rough house. Okay, you want entertainment, I'll give you entertainment with a capital E. There's nothing I like better than discovering young talent. And I...

NICKY. Where did they discover you? Under a rock? Get on with it.

PROVOLONEY. *(Getting mad)* What I'm doing is laying the foundation for the evening at...

NICKY. You're laying an egg. *(EVERYONE laughs)*

PROVOLONEY. I've gotten big laughs from tougher crowds than you.

NICKY. Before or after you dropped your pants? *(EVERYONE laughs)*

PROVOLONEY. *(Furious)* That does it! I don't have to take this. Do your own stinkin' show. *(STAR CAT jumps up and soothes Provoloney's ego)*

STAR CAT. Aw, c'mon, he's just joshing you. You're doing great. Go on. Guys, give him some support. *(THEY applaud)*

PROVOLONEY. Well, if you insist. Without further ado *(HE gives Nicky a dirty look)* please give a warm hand to a sister act that ends all sister acts. Straight from exotic Siam, the spectacular, the inseparable, Hester and

Esther. Take if away girls.

(CHICKLET and BERDINE enter in a wild red siamese twin costume joined at the hip)

CHICKLET. My name is Ester.
BERDINE. My name is Hester.
BERDINE/CHICKLET. *(In unison)*
LIFE AIN'T ALWAYS A PIP
WHEN YOU'RE JOINED AT THE HIP.

IF JUST A SMALL BUMP
DOES STRANGE THINGS TO YOUR RUMP,

AND A HOT STRIPPER'S GRIND
REALLY ACHES YOUR BEHIND,

BUT ENUF OF THIS KVETCHING,
WE STILL LOOK MOST FETCHING,

SO VO DE OH DO,
LET'S GET ON WITH THE SHOW.
(CHICKLET and BERDINE begin singing a song such as "The Lady in Red."* In the middle of the song, CHICKLET begins talking to herself. BERDINE continues to sing.)
CHICKLET. Red...red...red dress. *(mutters)* Take that off. You look like a whore. Take that dress off. *(Cries like a baby)* I'm angry. I'm angry. I don't like this. I can't move.

---

*Note: Permission to produce PSYCHO BEACH PARTY does not *include permission to use this song. Producers are hereby cautioned that they must procure such permission the the copyright owner, Warner Bros., Inc., 9000 Sunset Blvd., Los Angeles, CA   90069.*

Get me out. *(BERDINE continues to sing nervously —
CHICKLET makes animal sounds)*

BERDINE. Chicklet, please. "The Lady in Red," the
fellas are crazy about the...

CHICKLET. *(Muttering)* Crazy, crazy, the fellas are
crazy...about ME! Me, Ann Bowman, live, onstage!
(Laughs raucously) At last, in the spotlight.

BERDINE. *(Nervously improvising)* Now Chicklet's going
to do some impersonations for you. Who are you
doing, Chicklet?

CHICKLET. *(As ANN)* Get your hands off me, you
blithering bull dyke.

BETTINA. What's going on?

CHICKLET. *(As ANN)* Silence! Now that I have your
attention, I'd like to sing my song, my SOLO! *(Crooning)*
More than the greatest love the world has known... *(A
LITTLE GIRL)* Stop, I don't like your singing, you scare
me. *(As ANN)* Shut up you little bitch! *(As TYLENE)* Don't
you be talking to that chile like that. *(As ANN)* Do not
underestimate my fury, Tylene. *(As TYLENE)* I ain't
scared of you, mother. *(As DR. ROSE MAYER)* Excuse me,
if I may interject. This is Dr. Rose Mayer speaking. If you
have a personal grievance, by all means you are entitled
to a fair hearing but let us not air out our dirty laundry in
public. *(As ANN)* Butt out, you blabbering battleax. *(As
DR. ROSE MAYER)* Once more I must interject. Ann, the
question I ask of you is why? Why cause all this tsouris,
this unhappiness. *(As ANN)* Enough! You insolent fools! I
am taking over Chicklet's mind once and for all. Chicklet
is officially dead!

BERDINE. Stop it, stop it!

CHICKLET. *(As ANN)* I warned you not to touch me. *(SHE starts to strangle Berdine. STAR CAT and KANAKA try to separate them. CHICKLET pulls out a straight razor and the chase in on. CHICKLET is on the rampage chasing all the kids, dragging Berdine behind her.)* It's a shave and a haircut for all of you. How about white sidewalls, honey. *(SHE moves toward BETTINA)* I'll get you anyway, Peewee.

BETTINA. *(Holding her ponytail)* It's a fake! It's a switch! Help! Help! *(STAR CAT and KANAKA subdue Chicklet. THEY pin her arms back and grab the razor. BERDINE is in hysterics.)*

STAR CAT. Let's get them out of that costume. *(THEY break away the siamese twin costume, freeing them. BETTINA comforts Berdine)*

(MRS. FORREST enters)

MRS. FORREST. I thought I'd find her here. I'm going to have all of you arrested for kidnapping.

STAR CAT. Mrs. Forrest, your daughter is mentally ill.

MRS. FORREST. My little girl is as normal as I am.

CHICKLET. *(In the voice of TYLENE)* I gotta go back to work at the Safeway.

MRS. FORREST. *(Near hysteria, grasping at straws)* She wants to be an actress. She's putting on a character. *(Breaks down)* She's not sick!

CHICKLET. *(An ANN)* You're so right, Mrs. Forrest, I am hardly the lunatic they are painting me to be. I am totally in control.

STAR CAT. You are merely a delusion of Chicklet

Forrest that enables her to express anger and rage.

CHICKLET. *(As ANN)* Fancy phrases. And a big basket. I'd like to strap you on sometime.

STAR CAT. That is highly unlikely since you are about to be obliterated.

CHICKLET. *(As ANN)* Party pooper.

STAR CAT. You don't frighten me. I'm flesh and blood. You're a psychological manifestation. I can conquer you.

CHICKLET. *(As Ann)* There's no man alive strong enough to conquer me...maybe Bob Hope.

STAR CAT. I'm going to place you under hypnosis and through the technique of past regression get to the root of the trauma that fragmented Chicklet's personality.

MRS. FORREST. I can't allow this. He doesn't know what he's doing.

PROVOLONEY. He's had three semesters of psychiatric training.

STAR CAT. Look into my eyes. I'm taking you back in time.

MRS. FORREST. Someone stop this madness!

CHICKLET. *(As ANN)* Oh shut your hole. Go on darling Doctor Star Cat.

STAR CAT. I want to speak to Chicklet. Chicklet, are you there?

CHICKLET. It's hard, I feel so far away, I can't... *(SHE begins to sound like a radio with static)*

MRS. FORREST. She's babbling. *(SHE exits)*

STAR CAT. It's a bad connection. Chicklet, I know you are there. We are here to help you. Trust me. Are you there? *(CHICKLET is sounding like a radio quickly switch-*

ing stations)

KANAKA. *(Sincerely)* Maybe you should try her on FM.

STAR CAT. Talk to us Chicklet, talk to us.

CHICKLET. *(Static noises clearing as DR. ROSE)* ...lieve you will have greater success conversing with one of us.

STAR CAT. Who am I talking to?

CHICKLET. *(As DR. ROSE)* Dr. Rose Mayer, you're on the air.

STAR CAT. Who exactly are you?

CHICKLET. *(As DR. ROSE)* A radio personality, and a syndicated columnist.

PROVOLONEY. This is weird, man, too weird.

CHICKLET. *(As DR. ROSE)* I serve a very important function in Chicklet's life. Any situation that gets a little mishugga, that requires tact or diplomacy, I come in. In toto, I'm a people person.

STAR CAT. And who is Tylene?

CHICKLET. *(As TYLENE)* I am her ambitious self. Come September first, I am attending night school where I can study keypunch and office management skills.

(Suddenly CHICKLET turns into STEVE, an all American boy.)

CHICKLET. *(As STEVE)* Whoa, can I just say something for a minute?

STAR CAT. I believe we're meeting someone new. What's your name?

CHICKLET. *(As STEVE)* Steve.

STAR CAT. Are you also a radio personality?

CHICKLET. *(As STEVE)* No. I'm a male model.

STAR CAT. Describe yourself.

CHICKLET. *(As STEVE)* I'm a forty regular. *(Fidgety)* I'm very important to Chicklet. I'm her athletic self. I enjoy all sports, ice hockey, kayaking, golf, competition bowling. Of course I do try to be a well-rounded person. I love old romantic movies, snuggling up by a fire. I guess what I look most for in a girl are great legs and a sense of herself. *(HE winks at Bettina, who gasps)*

STAR CAT. Are there any more of you?

CHICKLET. *(As STEVE)* Gosh, let's see, there's a veterinarian, a couple singers, a reformed rabbi, a lighting designer, the accounting firm of Edelman and Edelman, a podiatrist... *(As CHICKLET)* Help me.

STAR CAT. Chicklet, is that you?

CHICKLET. *(As A LITTLE GIRL)* Uh huh. *(SHE sings)* "IT' RAINING, IT'S POURING..."

STAR CAT. How old are you?

CHICKLET. Eight. Seven and a half.

STAR CAT. Where are you?

CHICKLET. In a room, Mama calls it the hotel. There's a playground across the street. My brother Frankie and me like to go on the swings.

BERDINE. She doesn't have a brother.

CHICKLET. I do too have a brother. He's seven and a half.

YO YO. Twins.

CHICKLET. Mama says we can't go on the swings alone. She says it's too dangerous. Mama's going to take us to the movies today. She says she's gonna...

(MRS. FORREST appears in a strange light, SHE is in the past, dressed in a red dress like a sexy young whore in the 1940's)

MRS. FORREST. *(Gently)* Baby, I'm so sorry. We're gonna have to go to the movies another day. Mama's gotta work. Fellas, come on in. These are my twins, ain't they cute?

CHICKLET. But you promised you'd take us to the movies.

MRS. FORREST. Well, I'm sorry. What do you want from my life? You wanna eat, don'tcha? Anyways, we gotta do our bit for the boys who go overseas. These guys are in the Navy and your Mama is making sure they are very well entertained. *(SHE giggles. To the children)* Now darlings, go outside and play. I'll meet you in the playground in an hour.

CHICKLET. You're not fair.

MRS. FORREST. Florence, I don't want anymore lip. Take Frankie and go outside and play. And don't you go near those swings. *(SHE turns to the sailors)* Sorry guys, being a Mom ain't easy. Now what was your name again, good looking? Please to meetcha, Johnny. Just call me Ann. Ann Bowman. *(SHE exits)*

CHICKLET. *(In her normal voice)* I was so angry. I wanted to hurt her. I took Frankie's hand and we crossed the street to the playground. There were these awful slum children playing, pounding strange primitive instruments. A sharp breeze caused the wild flowers to have the wizened faces of starving circus clowns. The sky seemed so threatening, as if the clouds were created of demented angels warning me to flee. But I couldn't. I can't. Don't make me go on. Please.

STAR CAT. You must. What happened next?

CHICKLET. I look down and there's a pale green snake slithering along the crack of the pavement, a cooly seductive creature on its way to a lizard ball. This veridian temptress stops to deliver me a message. A perverse billet-doux that I must disobey my mother. No, no, I can't do that. I love my mother. She's kind and beautiful. The snakes multiply, in a moment, there are reptiles covering the jungle gym making those steel bars as green as grass and terrifyingly alive. And all of them whispering "Go on, go on, go on the swings. Your mother doesn't love you. She loathes the very sight of you." I looked at my little brother, wearing his red overalls with the little fishes. I said, "Frankie, let's go on the swings. It'll be fun. I don't care what Mama said." He got on the swing and I pushed him. Harder and harder I pushed him until he was soaring into the clouds and that's when I dared him. I dared him, "I bet you can't stay on with no hands." He took me up on the bet and let go, and my wonderful little twin brother, this adorable little boy who loved and trusted me, he flew off the swing and into the outstretched arms of those ghastly angels and I never saw him again until we found his crushed, little body in the dumpster next door!

(SHE dissolves into tears, STAR CAT holds her. MRS. FORREST appears again as she is today.)

MRS. FORREST. *(Devastated)* It's all true. All of it true. I was so ashamed. I blamed myself for the death of my boy. But I always loved my little girl. *(To CHICKLET)* You must believe that. I did love you. I do. And when Chicklet lost her memory of that day, I took it as a blessing from God. I vowed to create a new life for us. I changed my name, moved to a new city. I suppose I tried too hard, went too far and now...now I see I'm doomed to failure.

CHICKLET. Mother, hold me. *(THEY embrace)*

BERDINE. *(Sobbing)* I was supposed to be her best friend but I never knew.

KANAKA. How do you feel, Chicklet?

CHICKLET. As if a thousand doors have been opened.

PROVOLONEY. But what does this all mean?

STAR CAT. It's really very simple. Chicklet did her best to suppress this traumatic childhood episode by denying herself all normal human emotion, so she created various alter egos to express emotion for her. She associated the sex drive with her mother, so she in effect became her childhood vision of her mother, Ann Bowman, whenever placed in a potentially erotic situation.

KANAKA. Is this condition contagious?

STAR CAT. Indeed not. Over eighteen percent of all Americans suffer from some form of multiple personality disorder. It is not communicable and in most cases, treatable with medical care.

BETTINA. *(Energetically)* This is the most exciting story I've ever heard. This is the project that's going to win me an Oscar.

PROVOLONEY. Huh?

BETTINA. A surfer girl with a split personality. A prestige picture if I ever saw one. *(To Chicklet)* Honey, I want to option this property, and believe me I'll pay top dollar. I can't promise casting approval but you can trust my integrity.

MRS. FORREST. I don't know. This is an invasion of...

CHICKLET. Mother, this is important. I want the public to know what it's like to suffer from a multiple personality disorder. And Berdine, will she be in the picture? She's very important, you know.

BETTINA. Oh, sure, sure, a character part.

STAR CAT. But Bettina, do you really think you're ready to interpret such a complex role?

BETTINA. *(With artistic intensity)* I don't think, I feel. I know this girl. I feel her torment. I am Chicklet! *(Suddenly switching to her practical show business nature)* Yo Yo and Provoloney, I'm taking you to New York with me as technical consultants on the Malibu scene.

Yo Yo. Wow, New York!

PROVOLONEY. The Philharmonic!

Yo Yo. The New York City Ballet!

PROVOLONEY. Balanchine!

Yo Yo. The Frick! Provoloney, should we tell them about us?

PROVOLONEY. Yeah, since this is the time for truth telling. Yo Yo and I are lovers. *(EVERYONE gasps)*

Yo Yo. Yes, and we're proud of it. I've read all about the persecution of homosexuals, how in big cities, bars are raided and innocent people arrested, their lives ruined. But someday, someday we're going to fight back and the laws will be changed, and our brothers and sister will march down the main streets of American shouting that we are proud to be who we are!

PROVOLONEY. Oh, Yo Yo, I really love you. *(THEY embrace. The CROWD sighs in sympathy.)*

BETTINA. Come on everybody, let's move this party to my place. I've got the best record collection in town. *(THEY ALL hoot and holler and exit except for BERDINE)*

BERDINE. *(Alone onstage, holding the siamese twin costume)* Life sure is wacky. Here Chicklet and I were best friends and I never really knew her. If I don't know *her,* can I ever truly know anyone? Star Cat thinks science can tell us everything, and Bettina says if she feels things, they're true. Oh, sweet, lonely Schopenhauer and crazy ole Nietzsche and dear, committed Jean-Paul, all of you searching and never settling for an easy answer to life's eternal puzzlement. I hereby vow to carry on your never-ending quest. I know now that my true calling is to be a novelist and devote my life to exploring the fathomless possibilities of the human comedy. Hey, wait for Berdine! *(SHE runs off)*

BLACKOUT

SCENE TEN

The beach at twilight. STAR CAT is walking along the beach, wearing a tie and jacket. KANAKA enters carrying a suitcase.

KANAKA. Hey, my man. It's time to shove off. You gonna say farewell to your old chum, Kanaka?

STAR CAT. You off to Tahiti?

KANAKA. *(Embarrassed)* No, uh not Tahiti, exactly.

STAR CAT. The Ivory Coast?

KANAKA. New York.

STAR CAT. New York. What kind of place is that for the King of the Surfers?

KANAKA. Bettina. She wants me with her. She needs me.

STAR CAT. I had no idea. You and Bettina.

KANAKA. Yeah well, you know Bettina and her incredible instincts about people. She says our personalities sort of fit together like a crazy jigsaw puzzle. But I told her, I'm the kind of guy that needs my freedom. I don't put up with no bunk, no star tantrums.

(From offstage, we hear BETTINA shouting like a fishwife)

BETTINA. Kanaka! Don't keep me waiting! We've got a nine o'clock plane to catch and I'm not missing it on account of some slow as molasses beach bum. Move it!

KANAKA. *(Subservient)* Yes, Bettina. *(To Star Cat)* Ciaou, kid. *(HE exits)*

STAR CAT. *(To himself)* The great Kanaka. What a mystery.

(CHICKLET appears in a beautiful gown, somehow grown up and lovely)

CHICKLET. Good evening, Star Cat.

STAR CAT. *(In shock)* Chicklet?

CHICKLET. It's a beautiful night. The King of the Sea must be having cocktails.

STAR CAT. Chicklet, you've become a young woman.

CHICKLET. Have I? Star Cat, I...

STAR CAT. I'm not Star Cat anymore. Call me Herbert. Herbert Mullin. Everything seems so different now. I'm leaving the beach.

CHICKLET. Where are you going?

STAR CAT. Back to college. I think I could make a good psychiatrist.

CHICKLET. Do you really want to, with all your heart?

STAR CAT. I do. I want to make sure a monster like Ann Bowman never appears again.

CHICKLET. I'll miss you, Star Cat...I mean, Herb.

STAR CAT. I was wondering...would you wear my pin?

CHICKLET. *(Thrilled)* Your pin. Does this mean we're exclusive?

STAR CAT. Well, I'll be all the way in Boston. You can't expect a guy to...

CHICKLET. *(Mad)* Well, forget it, you creep. I'll be darned if I'll keep the home fires burning while you're pawing some Beacon Hill, blueblooded beasel.

STAR CAT. That sounds like Ann Bowman.

CHICKLET. I hope so.

STAR CAT. You're quite a girl. The only girl for me. So will you wear my pin?

CHICKLET. Will I ever! It's the ultimate. It positively

surpasses every living emotion I've ever had! *(SHE whirls around and takes his arm and THEY walk down the surf to their new happiness)*

BLACKOUT

SCENE ONE
ALTERNATE BEGINNING

The beach. YO YO and NICKY are playing with a beach ball, but staring at a girl out front.

Yo Yo. Nicky, look at that chick in the white bikini. She really knows how to shake those maracas.

NICKY. Look at that butt.

Yo Yo. Summer gives me a one track mind.

(PROVOLONEY enters.)

PROVOLONEY. Girls! Girls! Girls!

Yo Yo. Hey there, Provoloney!

PROVOLONEY. What a fantabulous day.

NICKY. Aw shoot, I gotta go get back to work at that malt shop. My lunch break is almost over.

Yo Yo. Call in sick.

PROVOLONEY. Say you were run over by a hit-and-run surfer.

NICKY. Nah, old Augie's a great guy. I couldn't let him down.

(STAR CAT enters.)

Yo Yo. Hey, Star Cat, how's my man?

81

STAR CAT. What are you clowns doing? Those waves are as high as Mount Everest.

PROVOLONEY. *(Looks out.)* Oh wow, look at them, man.

STAR CAT. It's time to hit the water.

NICKY. It's more BLT's for me. See ya, fellas. Gosh, I'm so happy! *(Exits.)*

STAR CAT. Come on guys, grab your boards, it's time to shoot the curl.

PROVOLONEY. Hot diggity! *(THEY ALL run offstage.)*

AUTHOR'S NOTE

In the original production I played Chicklet in drag. As I've said, this is not necessary. With a girl in the role, one cut in the script is advised.

SCENE ONE

BERDINE. You will, you will.

MARVEL ANN. We're in luck. Look at those four gorgeous hunks of male, over there, almost enough for second helpings. Now, a maneuver like this takes technique. Talk to me. Don't let them think we're looking at them.

PROPERTY LISTS

SCENE ONE:
Beach balls
Surf board
Coffee mug
Sunglasses
3 beach bags
Beach blanket
Berdine's parasol
Plastic spider

SCENE TWO:
Jock strap

SCENE THREE:
Diary with pencil attached

SCENE FOUR:
Beach bag
Beach blanket

SCENE SIX:
Telegram
Cigarette
Cigarette holder

SCENE EIGHT:
Stool with straps attached
Ropes for binding Chicklet

TV tray with meal
Sheets tied together

SCENE NINE:
Limbo stands
Limbo poles
Oversized switchblade
Bongo drums

SCENE TEN:
Suitcase

COSTUME PLOT

CHICKLET
SC. 1:

    Black multi-colored dot smock
    Matching panties
    Purple and lavender beach mules
    CHANGE TO:
    Matching dot halter top

SC. 2:

    ADD:
    Second identical dot smock

SC. 4:

    REMOVE:
    Smock

SC. 6:

    Pink, yellow, and blue plaid pleated sailor smock
    Lavender lace ruffle panties
    Red feather boa

SC. 9:

    Pale lavender terrycloth mini-sunsuit
    Right hand: red jewelled evening glove
    High heels:
       Right foot: red
       Left foot: shell pink
    Right side of red spandex and sequin "Siamese twin" dress

SC. 10:

    Lavender and pale blue satin and tulle prom gown

    Lavender heels

    Pink flower wrist corsage

BERDINE

SC. 1:

    Straw "coolie" hat with lavender ribbons

    Purple and blue print cotton jacket with animal pins and brooches

    White and black polka dot sleeveless blouse

    White, pink, and blue floral print pedal pushers

    White gloves

    Pink socks

    Blue and magenta floral print deck shoes

SC. 3:

    White, pink, and light blue print pajama top with white fur collar

    Pink print pajama pants with white fur cuffs

    Purple terrycloth slippers

SC. 4:

    REPEAT:

    Sc. 1 polka dot blouse, pedal pushers, socks and shoes

SC. 6:

    Pink straw hat

    Black and magenta silk oriental jacket with animal pins and brooches

White and magenta "fish" print pedal pushers
Sc. 1 socks and shoes

SC. 8:
> *REPEAT:*
> Sc. 3 pajama costume
> *ADD:*
> Blue and white print curler cap
> *CHANGE:*
> Remove pajama top
> Add dark purple baseball jacket

SC. 9:
> Pale lavender terrycloth mini-sunsuit
> Lavender lace ruffle panties
> Left hand: red jewelled evening glove
> High heels:
>> Right foot: shell pink
>> Left foot: red
> Left side of red spandex and sequin "Siamese twin"
> dress

CURTAIN CALL:
> Repeat Sc. 1 costume without hat and gloves

MRS. FORREST
SC. 2:
> Sheer-to-waist "nude" panty hose
> Flesh tone stretch lace "Merry Widow" corset
> Pointed bust pads
> White and green print shift dress

Pale pink embroidered organza apron
Bright pink rubber gloves
Large chartreuse bead necklace
Chartreuse and gold earbobs
Large emerald ring
High heels:
    Right foot: silver with green polka dots
    Left foot: green with silver polka dots

SC. 7:

Green and yellow floral print taffeta "bubble"
    dress
Pink "A-line" coat with large shawl collar
Repeat Sc. 2 heels
"Harlequin" sunglasses.
Repeat Sc. 2 earbobs

SC. 8:

REMOVE:
Sunglasses and coat

SC. 9:

Remove corset and Sc. 8 costume
Remove earbobs
Underdress red stretch lycra "Ann Bowman" gown
    with bust pads and rear skirt hem velcroed up
Overdress grey and pink floral print cocktail dress
    with white collar and cuffs
White, pink, and black floral print high heels
Rhinestone bracelet

CHANGE:
    Remove cocktail dress and bust pads
    Unvelcro skirt of red gown
    Add Chicklet's Sc. 6 red feather boa
CHANGE:
    Reverse procedure into previous cocktail dress

BETTINA
SC. 4:
    Black stretch lace "Merry Widow" corset with bust pads
    Black sheer-to-waist panty hose
    Black velvet one-piece bathing suit
    Large "Italian" pink and blue metallic on clear plastic hat with braided wig chignon and pink and blue chiffon drape
    Black evening gloves with jet stones
    Large amethyst bracelets
    Rhinestone "Empress" necklace
    Rhinestone and jet rings
    Large rhinestone eardrops
    Black patent leather high heels
    Large "Harlequin" bird-wing sunglasses

SC. 6:
    Black stretch knit top with off-the-shoulder band of rhinestone, jet, and silver spangles
    Black stretch knit toreador pants
    Black and white polka dot stretch belt with black sequins
    Sc. 4 heels

Sc. 4 eardrops
Sc. 4 corset

SC. 9:

Repeat Sc. 4 corset
Orange and black "Tiger" striped strapless tor-
    eador top
Matching stripe toreador pants
Black organza overskirt with rhinestones on a black
    stretch sequin belt
Magenta and blue flower armbands
Lei
Sc. 4 necklace, earrings, and heels

MARVEL ANN
SC. 1:

Hip padding on dance briefs
"Nude" support tights
"Nude" sheer-to-waist panty hose
Yellow and green chainette fringe one-piece halter
    bathing suit with snap-in bust prosthesis
Magenta chiffon neck scarf
Yellow trimmed sailor hat
Large shell and topaz bracelet
Yellow green heels with pink bows

SC. 9:

Repeat Sc. 1 costume with shaved bald pate
ADD:
Bright blue oriental silk brocade robe

DEE DEE
SC. 1:
>   Black and magenta floral print bikini
>   White deck shoes

SC. 9:
>   Orange and blue stripe bikini with beading and
>   rhinestones
>   Floral print on clear plastic mini circle skirt with
>   rhinestones and ball fringe
>   Lei
>   Sc. 1 shoes

STAR CAT
SC. 1:
>   Coral choker
>   Mauve ragged clamdiggers
>   Brown stretch belt
>   Dark blue deck shoes
>   *CHANGE:*
>   Entrance with Marvel Ann: add magenta
>   Hawaiian shirt

SC. 4:
>   Repeat Sc. 1 costume without shirt

SC. 6:
>   Repeat
>   *ADD:*
>   Green Hawaiian shirt

SC. 9:
> Pink and yellow plaid slacks
> Lavender shirt with rhinestones and matching
>   plaid trim
> Light blue socks
> White buckskin loafers
> Lei

SC. 10:
> Remove shirt and lei
> *ADD:*
> "In-one" pink sportcoat, white shirt, and grey print
>   tie

KANAKA
SC. 1:
> Distressed, ragged blue jeans
> Leather thong and wood bead belt
> Ragged orange fishnet top
> Ragged white embroidered yoke Mexican shirt
> Brown beach thongs
> Sunglasses
> *CHANGE:*
> Entrance with Marvel Ann: remove white shirt

SC. 4:
> Repeat
> *REMOVE:*
> Orange fish net top

SC. 7:
> *ADD:*
> Fishnet top

SC. 9:
> Black silk pleated pants
> Black leather mirror-studded belt
> White ragged steward's jacket with rhinestones, gold bugle beaded trim, and gold epaulets with grass fringe—painted Hawaiian "scene" on back
> White socks
> Black high-top tennis shoes

SC. 10:
> *REMOVE:*
> Jacket and lei
> *ADD:*
> Black sheer shirt

CURTAIN CALL:
> Repeat Sc. 9 costume

PROVOLONEY
SC. 1:
> Yellow and orange print jams
> Fuschia and purple propellor beanie with buttons
> Yellow socks
> Pink high-top tennis shoes

SC. 4:
 REMOVE:
 Beanie

SC. 5:
 ADD:
 Purple and orange print terrycloth lined sleeve-
  less top

SC. 6:
 REMOVE:
 Terrycloth top
 ADD:
 Black and gold cummerbund
 Black and gold tux jacket
 Blue and magenta print neckscarf
 Straw snap-brim with orange and purple pom-
  pom band
 Sunglasses

SC. 9:
 Orange and yellow Hawaiian shirt with bugle
  beads and rhinestones
 Blue print bathing trunks with rhinestones
 Lei

YO-YO
SC. 1:
 Orange and blue green print bikini briefs
 Yellow socks
 Orange high-tops

SC. 5:

> White cut-off T-shirt with red, black and purple
> trim
> Pale lavender cut-off stretch football pants with red
> and black trim
> Repeat Sc. 1 shoes and socks

SC. 9:

> Orange and yellow "frog" print stretch clam-
> diggers with rhinestones
> No shirt
> Lei

NICKI
SC. 1:

> Orange floral banded tank top
> Lavender bathing trunks with black and white
> check trim
> White socks
> White high-top tennis shoes

SC. 9:

> Lavender fish printed polo shirt with bugle bead
> trim and rhinestones
> White, blue, and orange print jams with rhine-
> stones
> Repeat Sc. 1 socks and shoes

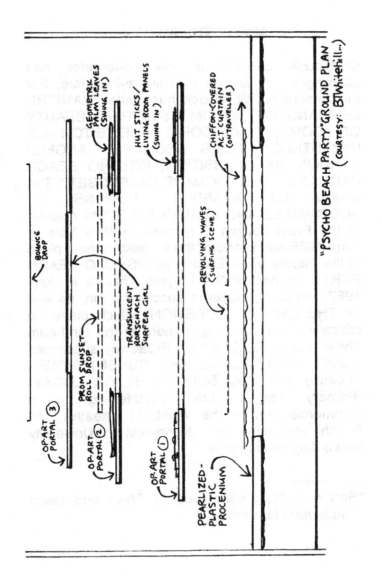

OP-ART PORTAL (3)

BOUNCE DROP

PROM SUNSET ROLL DROP

OP-ART PORTAL (2)

GEOMETRIC PALM LEAVES (SWING IN)

TRANSLUCENT RORSCHACH SURFER GIRL

HUT STICKS / LIVING ROOM PANELS (SWING IN)

OP-ART PORTAL (1)

REVOLVING WAVES (SURFING SCENE)

CHIFFON-COVERED ACT CURTAIN (ON TRAVELLER)

PEARLIZED-PLASTIC PROCENIUM

"PSYCHO BEACH PARTY" GROUND PLAN

(COURTESY: B.T. Whitehill...)

ABOUT THE AUTHOR

CHARLES BUSCH is the co-founder and playwright-in-residence of Theatre-in Limbo. For this ensemble, Mr. Busch has written VAMPIRE LESBIANS OF SODOM,* SLEEPING BEAUTY OR COMA,* THEODORA: SHE BITCH OF BYZANTIUM, TIMES SQUARE ANGEL,* PARDON MY INQUISITION, PSYCHO BEACH PARTY,* and RED SQUARE ON SUNSET.* The double bill, VAMPIRE LESBIANS OF SODOM/SLEEPING BEAUTY OR COMA opened at the Provincetown Playhouse in New York in June 1985 and is one of the longest running plays in the history of off-Broadway. PSYCHO BEACH PARTY opened at the Players Theatre in July, 1987 and also enjoyed a successful run, as well as THE LADY IN QUESTION* which played a critically acclaimed engagement at the Orpheum Theatre in 1989. Other Off-Broadway successes include RED SCARE ON SUNSET* (WPA Theatre) and YOU SHOULD BE SO LUCKY* (Primary Stages, later transferring to a commercial run at the Westside Theatre). Mr. Busch graduated from Northwestern University with a degree in drama.

----

*See our *Basic Catalogue of Plays* and latest *Supplement* for details.

THE DIVINE SISTER
Charles Busch

Comedy / 1m, 5f
The Divine Sister is an outrageous comic homage to nearly every
Hollywood film involving nuns. Evoking such films as *The Song
of Bernadette, The Bells of St. Mary's, The Singing Nun* and *Agnes of
God, The Divine Sister* tells the story of St. Veronica's indomitable
Mother Superior who is determined to build a new school for
her Pittsburgh convent. Along the way, she has to deal with a
young postulant who is experiencing "visions," sexual hysteria
among her nuns, a sensitive schoolboy in need of mentoring, a
mysterious nun visiting from the Mother House in Berlin, and a
former suitor intent on luring her away from her vows.

This madcap trip through Hollywood religiosity evokes the
wildly comic but affectionately observed theatrical style of the
creator of *Die, Mommie, Die!* and *Psycho Beach Party.*

"Cue the "Hallelujah" chorus! Charles Busch has put on a
nun's habit and is talking to God, from whom he has evidently
received blessed counsel. *The Divine Sister*, his new comedy
at the SoHo Playhouse, finds Mr. Busch at peak form. This
gleefully twisted tale of the secret lives of nuns — in which the
playwright doubles as leading lady — is Mr. Busch's freshest,
funniest work in years, perhaps decades."
–The New York Times

OTHER TITLES AVAILABLE FROM SAMUEL FRENCH

DIE MOMMIE DIE!
Charles Busch

Comic Melodrama / 3m, 3f / Interior

This comic melodrama evokes the 1960's movie thrillers that featured such aging cinematic icons as Bette Davis, Joan Crawford, Lana Turner and Susan Hayward. Faded pop singer, Angela Andrews is trapped in a corrosive marriage to film producer, Sol Sussman. In her attempt to find happiness with her younger lover, an out of work TV star, Angela murders her husband with the aid of a poisoned suppository. In a plot that reflects both Greek tragedy as well as Hollywood folklore, Angela's resentful daughter, Edith, convinces Angela's emotionally disturbed son, Lance, to avenge their father's death by killing their mother. Lance, demanding proof of Angela's crime, slips some LSD into her after-dinner coffee, triggering a wild acid trip that exposes all of Angela's dark secrets.